BARBARA WEBB

Beginners Book
of Navigation

WARD LOCK LIMITED

© 1975 Barbara Webb

ISBN 0 7063 1680 0

First published in Great Britain 1975 by Ward
Lock Limited, 116 Baker Street, London, W1M
2BB

Designed by Andy Vargo

Computer Typesetting by Print Origination,
Bootle, Lancs, L20 6NS

Printed in Great Britain by Hollen Street Press
Ltd., Slough

Contents

Introduction

This book is written as an introduction to a fascinating art—the art of navigation. Undoubtedly the most satisfactory way of starting to learn to navigate is to sail with an experienced person. He will explain to a beginner how the objects that he can see around the boat are marked on charts, how he can use a hand-bearing compass, how to look up tide tables and use tidal stream atlases, and so on. The crew absorbs all this sort of information, gains confidence in his ability to use charts and publications, and only later starts to learn how to plot courses and sail safely from A to B.

An increasing number of people to-day who buy a boat and go sailing tend to learn from their own mistakes rather than from an experienced companion. The first eleven chapters of this book give the information that a new boat-owner would acquire from such a companion. This is the ground-work of navigation, the basic facts that every skipper must know for day sailing, especially in waters that are strange to him. Imagine a sailor, used to the gentle tidal streams that are found in the broad sweep of bay where he normally sails, who then goes out in an estuary where the ebb stream reaches 7 knots. He may win all the races in his home waters, but unless he keeps his eyes and ears open he could well be in trouble when that ebb really gets going.

Many people carry a compass on board before they have learnt to navigate properly. It can be of great help provided it is used within the limitations of their knowledge, and provided the information it gives them is correctly applied. Wrongly used it can lead them into danger.

The remaining chapters cover plotting courses, fixing the boat's position, dead reckoning and passage planning. They are built on the foundation of the preceding chapters which will have been put into practice with increasing confidence every time a sailor has taken his boat out. Unfortunately there are many sailors around to-day who regard navigation as a black art too difficult for them to learn, and there are some who, irrespective of a lack of knowledge of navigation, embark on ambitious trips disregarding their own and others' safety. They know the ground-work backwards, but shy away from navigation proper.

Navigation is fun—in its simplest form as dealt with in this book it is by no means difficult and there is no reason at all for any skipper to say 'I can't'. All he needs to do is to be able to add and subtract and to take the trouble to understand when and why he does so, as explained in the later chapters of the book.

There is immense satisfaction in arriving safely at some distant destination and in becoming one of the most sought-after members of the sailing fraternity—a skilled navigator. In writing this book my grateful thanks are due to Capt. J. H. Mitton, R. N. (Retd.) for his valuable assistance in reading and checking the typescript.

1 : Before your first sail

Even before going on your very first sail in charge of a boat you will need to think about some of the first essentials of navigation. You will find out where you can sail safely, avoiding dangers both visible and hidden; you will find out how the water in which you will be sailing is moving; you will ask what the local rules are with which you must comply; you will listen to the weather forecast and decide whether it is the right day for your first sail.

Where you can sail safely. As you look round at a lake, reservoir or river the water appears most inviting—perhaps there is a twig or two sticking up here and there, perhaps you can see a fence stretching out towards the river, or perhaps you are setting out to sea from a broad sweep of beach. Dangers there are, and some of them can be seen, but some cannot. If you are sailing inland on a lake or a river there may be overhead cables or some overhanging trees in which you could catch the top of the mast; a little downstream of you there may be a weir; round the next bend there may be the trunk of a fallen tree submerged beneath the surface, a trap for the unwary and the uninformed; that fence may extend into the water; there may be a rusty roll of wire or a tangle of weeds which could catch the centreboard.

And if you are sailing at sea, your broad sweep of bay with its sunwarmed sands may end in a ledge of jagged rocks; there may be the remains of an old ruined jetty sticking out under the water, perhaps an old hulk left to rot in the mud.

As for the water, unless you are sailing on a still reservoir or a lake, the water itself will be moving, and often in both a horizontal and a vertical direction. If you are sailing on a river you will know that the current will accelerate as you approach a weir, and if the wind is light you could well be swept on to and over it unless you keep well clear. You will also know that in most places the current is stronger in the middle of a river than near the banks, and if you are making your way upstream you will try to avoid the stronger current. At sea it is more complicated because of the tides. You may launch your boat at high tide, and then find when you return after a sail that you can only get back on land by wading knee-deep through sticky mud. You will soon realise that the tidal stream does not always flow in the same direction; usually the flood stream sets one way, and the ebb stream the opposite way.

When it comes to local rules you should be sure that you know whether there is a local speed limit, especially if you are going out in a small fast motor-boat. There may be regulations which prohibit water-skiing close inshore among swimmers. In congested waters you may find generally accepted local customs for keeping clear of commercial traffic. If there are racing boats about, you will certainly need to keep well clear of them, and that means keeping far enough away to avoid interfering with their wind.

And then there's the weather. From the weather forecast you will know whether the likelihood is a nice sailing breeze, or whether you would do better to wait until the next day. Local fishermen and sailors, too, will have their own valuable comments to add, and these will be very useful to you.

So before setting out, go and talk to them. They will not sneer at you for asking advice, and they will much prefer to warn you of dangers than to have to rescue you from your predicament later. They were once beginners too! Ask them where the best place is for you to go and sail so that you will be out of the way of racing classes, whether there are any boats around that you should keep an eye open for—there may be a Hovercraft service which travels at much greater speed than other vessels, or a ferry which finds small boats a problem in restricted waters. They will tell you, too, of any patches of water which should be avoided because of eddies, they will tell you what the tidal stream will be doing and when it turns, and they will tell you whether the slip where you launched your boat or dinghy is accessible at all states of tide. What is more, if you have asked their advice and they know that you are either a beginner or a stranger to their waters, they will almost certainly keep a fatherly eye on you when you are out.

Navigation? Or common sense? Basically, navigation is common sense and observation, to which are added, as you extend your activities, a knowledge of how to use printed information about the waters you are sailing in, and some special equipment.

2 : Currents, tides and tidal streams

Before setting sail you must know in which direction the current or tidal stream will carry you, for otherwise you may find yourself unable to return home, or perhaps be swept on to some danger. Equally you must know the time of high and low water so that you will know the state of the tide when you are sailing.

From this it is evident that the word *tide* refers to the vertical movement of water as the level of the sea rises and falls, while *current* and *tidal stream* describe horizontal movement. You will come across the word tide used loosely to describe horizontal movement, particularly in speech but, correctly, tide refers only to vertical movement.

Currents behave very differently from tidal streams. Surface currents are horizontal movements of water due to a variety of natural causes, some known, some unknown. There are great ocean currents such as the Gulf Stream, currents in non-tidal waters such as the Baltic, and currents in rivers. They do not change direction according to a regular pattern as is the case with tidal streams. Two major causes of minor currents are wind and rain; a lot of rain in the higher reaches of a river will cause strong currents lower down, while a current at sea can be strengthened or reduced by a wind blowing with it or against it.

In narrow rivers currents tend to follow a basic pattern: they flow fastest away from the frictional braking effect of the banks and the bottom. In straight reaches the maximum speed is usually in the middle of the river where heavy spring rainfall or melting snows have swept a deep channel. Reaching a bend in the river the mass of water attempts to rush straight on, scouring the bottom near the bank and often undercutting it. The silt from the bottom and the bank is then carried suspended in the rushing water until the current slows, perhaps where it reaches the shallows on the inside of the next bend, or where the river spreads out into a broad estuary, or perhaps where it flows into the sea. As the silt drops it forms shallower patches, shoals or a bar at the entrance to a river (fig 1).

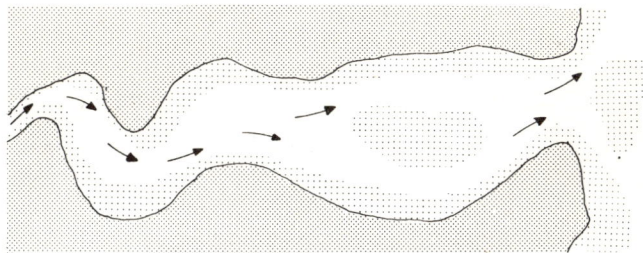

Fig.1 Shallows in the lower reaches of a river and a bar at the entrance.

Streams and small rivers are ideal places to learn about the effect of the coast on currents and tidal streams: twigs and leaves can be seen rushing past headlands, drifting more slowly along the bays, sometimes being carried upstream in backwaters behind a fallen tree, whirling around in a vortex behind rocks or speeding headlong through narrows and idling gently where the stream broadens out. All these have their counterparts at sea.

There are many currents in non-tidal areas such as the Baltic; their direction and rate cannot be predicted so accurately as those of tidal streams, but they are described in the *Pilots* issued by the Admiralty for each area, and charts also give details.

Tides. The level of the sea rises and falls regularly in response to the effects of the sun and the moon. Sitting on a British beach for some twelve and a half hours on a summer's day, starting, say, at half past nine, you can watch the full cycle (fig 2). The water's edge will gradually creep up the shore until, at high water at 15.40, it reaches a point rather below the line of flotsam flung up by the winter gales; after a short pause or *stand* it starts to recede, uncovering more and more of the sea-bed until, rather more than six hours later it pauses again before starting a new

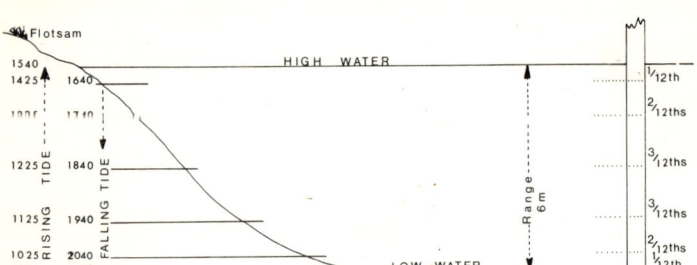

Fig.2 The full cycle of a tide.

cycle at 21.50. The highest point is reached at high water, and the greatest area of sea-bed is uncovered at low water. The vertical height difference between high water (HW) and low water (LW) is called the *range* and in figure 2 the range is 6 metres.

The water does not rise and fall at a constant rate. If the range of a tide is divided into twelfths the approximate rate can easily be remembered by the figures 1:2:3:3:2:1. Just before and after high and low water the rate is least, one-twelfth, like a car just starting or stopping. During the middle two hours when the car is running at full speed, the rate of rise or fall is greatest, 3/12ths per hour. So, in figure 2, the level falls ½ metre in the first hour, 1 metre in the second and 1½ metres in the third and so on. How this affects a boat sailing in shallow waters can be seen in figure 3, where again the range is 6 metres. The boat, which draws 1½ metres, can sail almost anywhere quite happily from 11.15 to 15.30, but only half an hour later, like the boat on the left, she is too close to the bottom for comfort. By 16.30 there is only one place she can sail safely, right in the middle of the channel.

Tides and the tidal streams are caused by the influence of the sun and the moon which attract the water particles. Twice a month their forces combine to cause particularly high levels at HW and lower than average levels at LW. These are the periods of *spring tides* when the range is greatest. Between springs the forces of the sun and moon gradually oppose each other more and more until, at *neap*

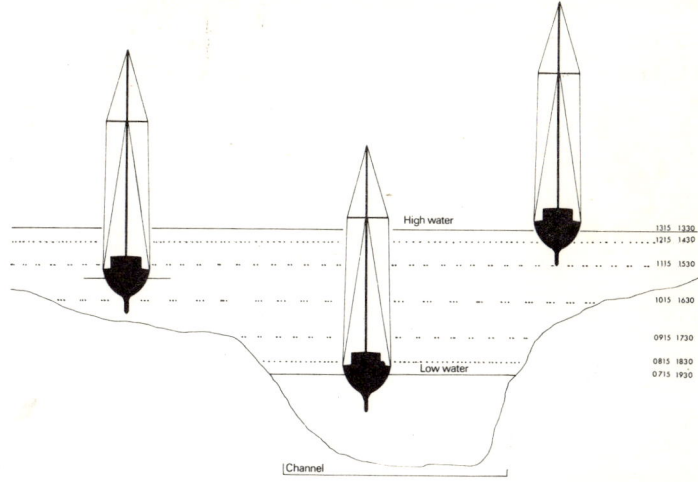

Fig.3 The rapid change in the water level during the middle two hours of the ebb makes a sudden difference to the area in which the boat can sail safely.

tides, the range is least with highest LW and lowest HW (fig 4).

The time of high water varies from day to day, but is rather under an hour later each day around the British coast, corresponding to the length of a lunar day which is 25 hours. This is why about a quarter of an hour is added at the top of the rising tide in figures 2 and 3. The amount of rise and fall differs greatly from place to place, from as

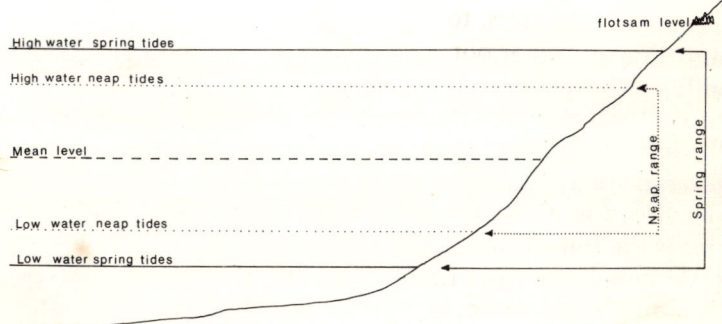

Fig.4 Spring and neap tides.

little as 1 metre to over 13 metres. There are also local peculiarities such as double low water at Portland, and double high water in the Solent area, and in such areas the 1:2:3:3:2:1 rule does not apply. Fortunately for the small boat sailor there are publications which make light work of deciding the times of high and low water, and we will learn how to use them in chapter 5. Each year the Admiralty publishes a list of predicted heights and time of tides. These, being predictions, can prove wrong in exceptional weather conditions such as in the case of the great floods of 1953 when strong gales caused the water in the southern part of the North Sea to rise far above the expected levels. Normally the differences in timing and height from those predicted are only slight.

Many ports and harbours publish their own tide tables. *Reed's Nautical Almanac* gives a full list for British and neighbouring waters, together with the tidal differences for places near a major port. Take Harwich for example: at Aldeburgh Ness HW occurs 1¼ hours before HW Harwich, while HW Pinmill is 21 minutes later than HW Harwich.

The predicted heights show whether it is springs or neaps. HW heights are greater at springs than at neaps, while low water heights are lower at springs. A typical table is shown at Appendix I and we shall use tide tables in chapter 5.

Tidal Streams. Tidal streams, too, are due to the effects of the sun and the moon; like the tides they react more vigorously at springs and are weakest at neaps. Their direction and strength are partly predictable, but are also influenced by the weather of the moment. Around the British Isles the tidal stream usually flows in one direction for something under six hours before slackening and then reverses for a similar period. During the period of change the direction is often uncertain and the rate is minimal; this is the time of *slack water*.

Although tides and tidal streams are closely linked, slack water rarely coincides with the time of HW. Often the rate follows the same sort of pattern as the rise and fall of a tide, with the greatest rate half way between the two slack waters. Strength and direction are very variable, however, and very much influenced by the coastline. For example, where a large harbour fills and empties through a narrow entrance the water rushes in and out extremely fast when the incoming and outgoing streams are at their maximum. There are many races off heads and promontories such as the famous Portland Race south of Portland Bill, and a narrow passage betwen an island and the mainland often experiences an accelerated rate, such as in the Alderney Race. Generally, tidal streams are slacker in broad sweeping bays, while behind promontories they often circle back against the main direction—in fact, they behave much like currents in streams.

The more complicated the coast with offshore islands or shoals, the more complex are the tidal streams. The Admiralty publishes *Tidal Stream Atlases* giving the set and rate at hourly intervals. *Reed's* also has a very useful series of chartlets for British waters, and some typical chartlets are shown at Appendix 2.

These chartlets give a general indication of the set and rate of the tidal stream but there are, of course, many local quirks and peculiarities which can only be learnt by experience. Generally the rate is least very close to the land, and this can be useful if you are sailing against a foul tidal set.

The rate of a tidal stream is given in *knots.* One knot equals one nautical mile per hour.

Other sources of information about tidal streams are the *Admiralty Pilots.* They give the rate and set for many places along the coasts and draw attention to any special dangers such as races, overfalls or tide-rips. Charts are very useful too. Where you see a capital letter printed inside a diamond ⟨A⟩, you will find somewhere on the chart a table giving the set and rate for each hour at that particular place.

All these publications cover great areas of water and, for that reason, can only give the major dangers and trends. Observation and experience of local waters should never be forgotten: a mental note of strange eddies in the water on a calm day could well save you from sailing into a

particularly vicious patch of sea on a very windy day. If
there is a race off a head near your home port, watch it
from the shore on a rough day and see how its position
changes when the tidal stream turns.

Using tidal streams to help your progress in a sailing
boat is a most rewarding pastime: you can cover a far
greater distance much more comfortably if you use them
intelligently, and they add more than a touch of spice to
sailing in salt water. Remember that wind against tidal
stream causes bigger and more vicious waves, and that in
shallow water waves become steeper and break more
easily. So play your tidal streams accordingly.

When you think that you know the tidal streams in your
area, find the hottest racing class there is and offer to crew
for the wiliest and most experienced skipper of the bunch.
You will learn more in one race than in three years'
cruising on your own—and you will almost certainly find
that even he acknowledges that he still has a lot to learn.

3 : The rule of the road

As soon as you leave the shore you see other boats
manoeuvring in the area—speedboats, other sailing boats
and perhaps even a ferry or a gigantic oil tanker. To avoid
collisions a knowledge of the rule of the road is essential—
the Highway Code of the sea. In a narrow channel two
boats heading towards each other cannot risk the sort of
comic dance that sometimes happens on pavements when
two people politely try to avoid each other, first to one
side, then to the other, before finally coming to a dead
stop, face to face, with sheepish grins. Instead a skipper
must react immediately and correctly to avoid a collision,
knowing that the other boat will also take the right action.

When it is your duty to do so it is important to
alter course in good time, making it quite clear to the
other boat what your intentions are. In a small boat this
means keeping a wary eye open all the time and

remembering that boats move at vastly different speeds. A small boat sailing at one knot in light airs will cover about 340 yards in 10 minutes, but in that same ten minutes an approaching steamer doing 15 knots will cover 2½ miles, so if you have to cross a busy shipping lane don't only check close at hand but look out for ships several miles away.

The International Regulations for Preventing Collisions at Sea. This is the official title for the rule of the road, and in indexes it often appears simply as Collisions, Regulations for preventing. A full copy should be carried on all boats; it is surprising how often you need to look something up. They are printed in *Reed's*.

Vessels are divided into two classes, those that are dependent *only* on the wind for propulsion, i.e. sailing vessels, and those that move independently, i.e. power-driven vessels. Note that word *only*, because the moment a boat uses her engine she is classed as power driven, whether her sails are up or not. When a sailing boat is using her engine and has her sails up the regulations state that she should carry a black cone forward, point downwards.

Fig.5 Power driven vessels approaching each other in virtually opposite directions must both alter course to starboard.

Two power vessels. When two power vessels approach each other from virtually opposite directions and would be likely to collide head on *both* must alter course to starboard (fig. 5).

When two power vessels are crossing each other and likely to collide only *one* must alter course. The vessel which sees that the other one is on her starboard side must alter course to keep out of her way (fig 6).

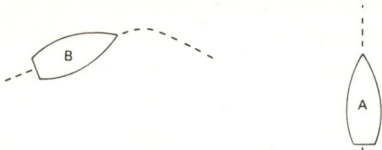

Fig.6 Power driven vessels crossing and likely to collide. The vessel which sees the other on her starboard side must alter course.

It is just as essential for boat *A*, with right of way, to keep steadily on course and to maintain her speed as it is for boat *B* to alter course to keep clear of her. In the illustration, if *A* slowed suddenly, *B* would have to make a very violent alteration of course to avoid a collision.

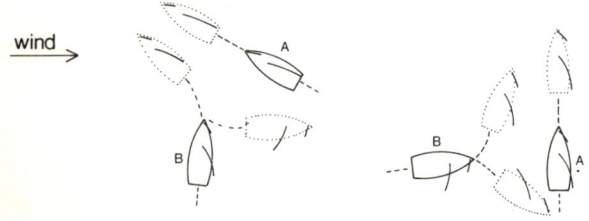

Fig.7 Sailing boats on the same tack. Windward boat gives way.

Two sailing vessels. If two sailing boats are likely to collide, first check whether both boats are on the same tack. If they are, and therefore both have the wind on the same side, it is up to the windward boat to keep out of the way (fig 7). *A* maintains course and speed as best she can while *B* can either luff up or pass astern of her before resuming her original course.

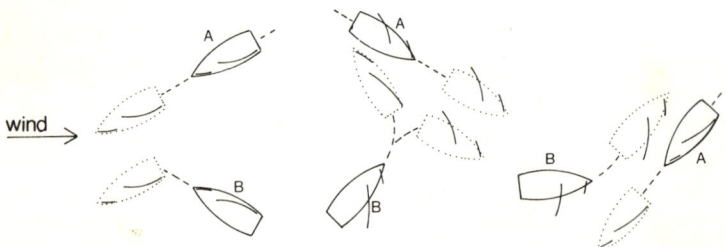

Fig.8 Sailing boats on opposite tacks. Port tack gives way.

On the other hand the two boats may be sailing on opposite tacks. Boat *B* on port tack, with the wind on her port side, must keep out of the way of boat *A* on starboard tack, and boat *A* must maintain course and speed so as not to baulk the boat giving way (fig 8).

Racing rules. Special rules come into force when sailing boats are racing. The best thing is to give all boats flying a square racing flag a really wide berth. They won't bless you if you get in their way.

Power and sailing vessels meeting. The basic rule is that power gives way to sail. A small motor boat is often easier to manoeuvre than a sailing boat, especially one with a spinnaker set. But, and it is a big *but,* there are countless occasions when a small yacht is far more manoeuvrable than a large power driven vessel. The international regulations specifically state that a sailing vessel must not hamper a power driven vessel in a narrow channel, and that sailing vessels must keep out of the way of fishing vessels. Common sense and courtesy should cause the sailing man to keep out of the way in very many other cases too. Sailing is a leisure sport which surely should not take precedence over commercial interests. To force an enormous oil tanker off course for the satisfaction of proving that power gives way to sail is as senseless as to bring a juggernaut lorry screeching to a halt at a pedestrian crossing—and can be just as dangerous too, for the sea directly ahead of the bow of many large tankers is hidden by the bows from the view of those on the bridge.

Overtaking. The definition of an overtaking vessel should be known. An overtaking vessel is one which comes up with another vessel from any direction more than 22½° (2 points) abaft her beam. Whether power driven or under sail an overtaking vessel must keep out of the way of the overtaken vessel until she is past and clear.

Narrow channels. As on the continent, you drive on the right! In other words, keep to starboard.

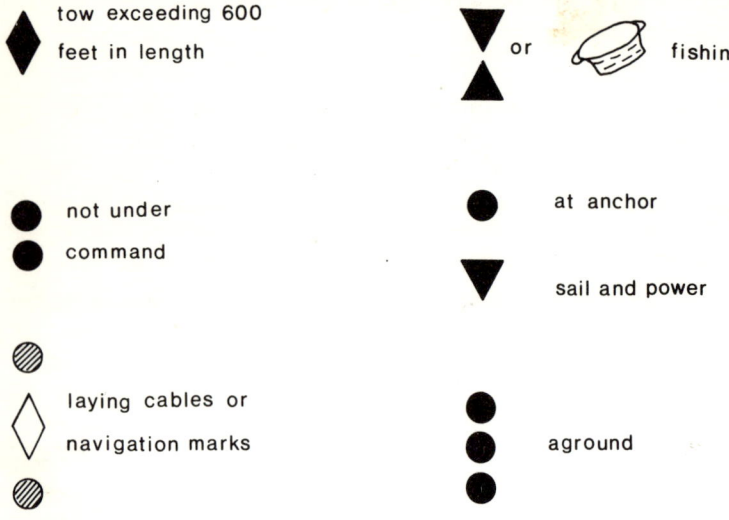

Fig.9 Special shapes carried in the rigging.

Special Vessels. Some vessels fly a variety of shapes in the rigging to draw attention to the fact that they will not be behaving normally or are a danger to other shipping (fig 9).

Sound signals. Vessels manoeuvring in sight of each other sometimes give sound signals to indicate what they are doing:

One short blast means 'I am altering course to starboard'.

Two short blasts means 'I am altering course to port'.

Three short blasts means 'My engines are going astern',

Five short blasts (or unofficially, a long drawn out blast) means 'Look out, get out of my way'.

Such are the *International Regulations*. To these add your own:

Keep a good look-out

Take avoiding action in good time and make your intentions clear

Sail with consideration for others

Don't 'die preserving your right of way'!

4 : A first look at charts

As soon as you venture further afield you find that you need more information than you can carry in your head. Try to find your way through a maze of country lanes following verbal instructions and you will soon need a map or have to stop to ask the way again. At sea you cannot usually stop a boat to ask the way—although I have been hailed by a man in a rowing boat in mid-Solent who asked for directions to the nearest shop!

Charts are the answer, and they have much in common with the more familiar Ordnance Survey maps, although they naturally concentrate on giving information about the water and only include those details of land that are of use to sailors. A map or a chart is a meaningless piece of paper until you have learnt how to interpret it, and you must be able to interpret it in two ways. First you must be able to find a visible object, say a lighthouse on your port bow, on the chart. Secondly, when you see something marked on the chart you must know what it is you are looking for as you scan the waters around the boat. A rock, for instance, hidden beneath the waves, is invisible to the man at the helm, but it is clearly marked on the chart, and so too is a buoy to seaward of the rock. By interpreting the chart correctly the helmsman knows when he sees the buoy that the rock lies between it and the shore, and therefore can steer clear of the danger.

There are no short cuts to learning how to read and interpret charts—all that is needed is practice. What is more, there is so much information on them that you need to study them again and again from different viewpoints—as we shall in the following chapters. First a look at some of those things which catch the eye immediately.

Admiralty Charts. Although private firms do print charts which are good and useful, it is only with Admiralty charts that we shall work in this book. They are unbeatable.

Types. There are two types of Admiralty chart available at present. The older ones are based on feet and fathoms and are called *fathoms charts,* while those of the newer series which is gradually replacing them are *metric charts.* The latter are clearly printed and much easier to read, which makes life much easier for a navigator working in a small boat in a big sea.

Colouring. The Admiralty fathoms charts show the land grey, deep water white, water under 6 fathoms blue and the foreshore, which covers and uncovers as the tide rises and falls, blue shaded with black dots or hatching, making it look darker than the sea beside it. The newer metric charts have buff-coloured land and a green foreshore while water under 5 metres deep is blue and deep water white. There is also a strip of blue along the shallower side of the 10-metre contour. On both charts magenta splashes draw attention to lights, and magenta is also used on metric charts for certain cautions, such as prohibited areas, separation zones, cable areas and so on.

Depth of water. Just as contour lines on Ordnance Survey maps join the points on land which are the same height above sea level, so depth contours connect points where the sea-bed is the same depth below sea level. The problem is, of course, that the sea does not stay at any one level for long, but rises and falls continuously. Soundings, therefore, all have to be related to the level of the sea at a specific state of the tide and, to reduce the danger of running aground to a minimum, they are usually related to a level as near as possible to the lowest likely to occur.

Chart Datum. The level below which soundings are given is called *Chart Datum.* It varies from chart to chart and from country to country, so it is essential to check under the title of the chart what level is being used. Fathoms charts are based on a number of different levels such as Mean Low Water Springs (MLWS). Metric charts are based on LAT (Lowest Astronomical Tides), the lowest level expected under normal meteorological conditions. Chart datum for tideless areas such as the Baltic is often Mean Sea Level (MSL).

Soundings on old charts are given in fathoms and feet, while the new issue is marked in metres and decimetres. It is *vital* to check which under the title of the chart you are using. You can imagine the result if you are sailing over a shoal in what you think is 2 fathoms; you suddenly hit the bottom with a crunch finding that in fact it is only 2 metres.

If you are using a metric chart but are mentally attuned to thinking of the draft of your boat in feet you may find yourself adjusting metres into feet. Multiply by three, and this will give you a few inches in hand because 1 metre = 3.28 feet. To convert metres to fathoms divide by 2 which gives you the rough figure, again on the safe side from the point of view of running aground.

Drying heights. When the tide is at the level of chart datum a great deal more of the sea-bed is uncovered than is the case at high water. All this ground which covers and uncovers is said to 'dry'. On a chart you will find some figures are underlined, and these are drying heights which show the height of that place above chart datum. Foreshore, shoals, banks, reefs, mud flats and rocks are shown in this way, underlined. Sometimes you will also find 'Dries 1 m.' New charts are metric, so the top of a rock marked $\underline{1}_2$ will be 1 metre 2 decimetres above sea level at low water LAT. Fathom charts give drying heights in feet: $\underline{4}$ = dries 4 feet.

Heights and contours on land. These are the heights and contours marked either on the grey part of fathoms charts or on the buff part of metric charts, and they are given above sea level at Mean High Water Spring Tides (MHWS) marked in feet or metres respectively.

Figure 10a shows an area on a fathoms chart, marked in feet and fathoms. A deep channel runs between the shore and a 12 ft. high rocky islet. There is a rock close by the islet which is awash at low water LAT, and a shoal patch, marked by a beacon, which dries 4 feet and which lies between the islet and the channel.

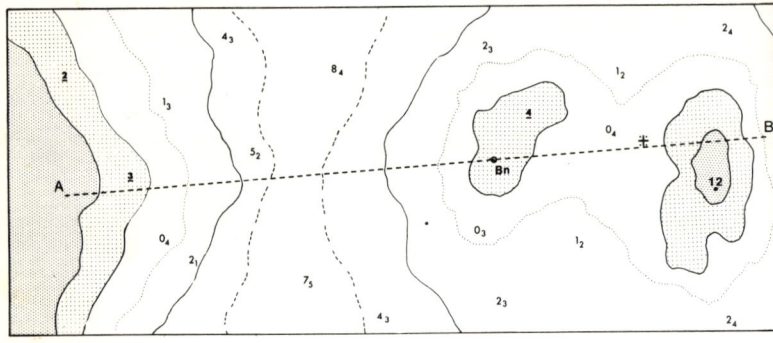

Fig.10a Part of a fathoms chart. Note that the height of the islet is given above MHWS, the drying heights which are underlined are given in feet above Chart Datum and the soundings are given in fathoms and feet below Chart Datum.

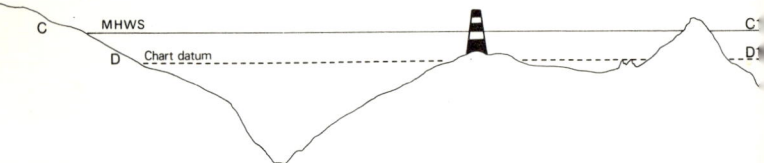

Fig.10b Cross section *AB* in fig 10a.

A cross section taken along the line *AB* would look like figure 10b. The line CC_1 represents the level of the water at MHWS when only the top of the islet, the beacon and the shore itself would be visible. To a boat approaching from the south at high water the channel would look something like figure 10c.

The lower line DD_1 represents the level of the water at chart datum, at which state of tide everything above DD_1 would be visible. There would be a greater expanse of shore, the shoal patch would be uncovered and the rock awash. The beacon would appear much higher. A boat approaching from the same spot would see a very much narrower channel looking roughly like figure 10d.

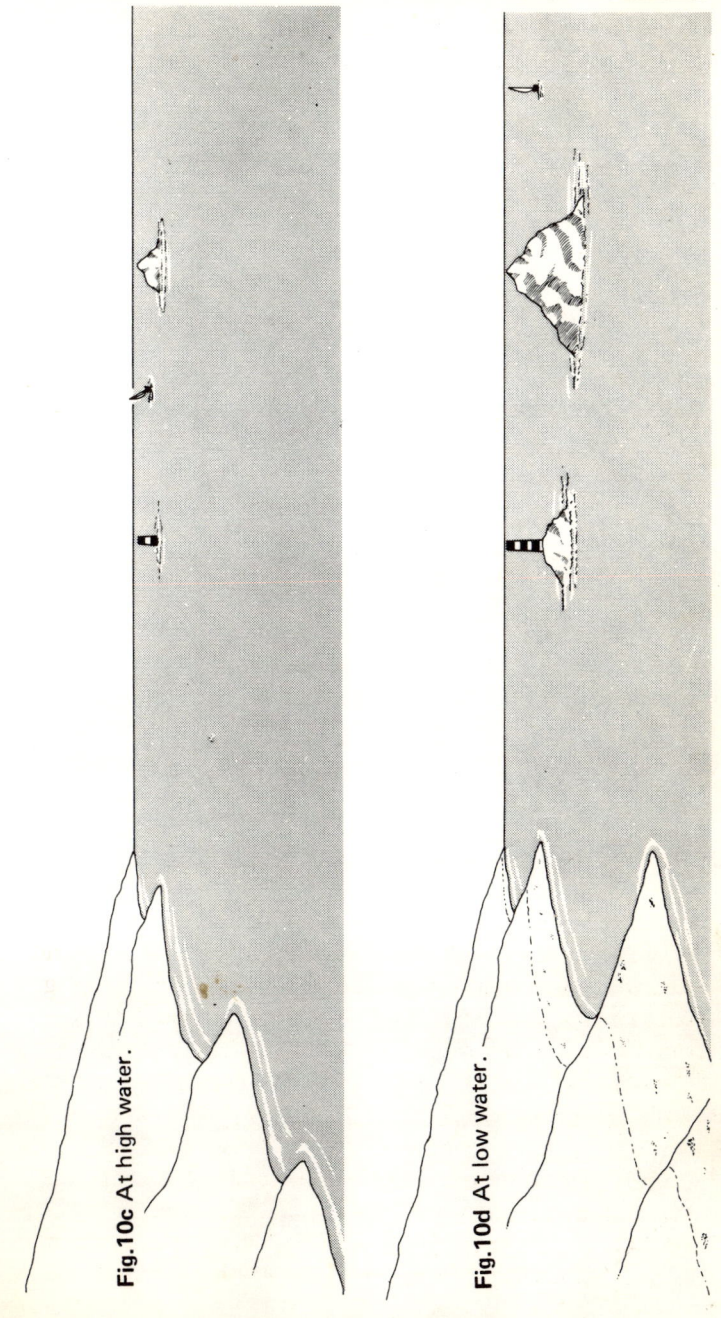

Fig.10c At high water.

Fig.10d At low water.

In this way the sailor can interpret the figures and contours on the chart into a three-dimensional picture. Checking the figures, and knowing the state of the tide when he is approaching an area, he is able to judge where he can sail safely. If it is near high water and his boat only draws 3 feet or so, he could sail quite close to the islet for he would not have to worry about the shoal. At or near low water he could only pass between the shoal and the islet in a very small boat drawing considerably less than 4 feet—the depth of water shown by the sounding 0_4. He would be wise to keep to the deep water side of the beacon unless he is sure that he has worked out the depth of water over the shoal really accurately.

Scale. Like maps, charts are drawn to different scales, and a good rule is to use the largest convenient scale for the area. There is room for more detail on a large scale chart than on a small scale one. Charts vary from very large scale for ports and harbour plans to very small scale covering part of an ocean.

Symbols and Abbreviations. *Admiralty Chart 5011*, which is actually a book, gives full details of the symbols and abbreviations which are used both on fathoms and metric charts.

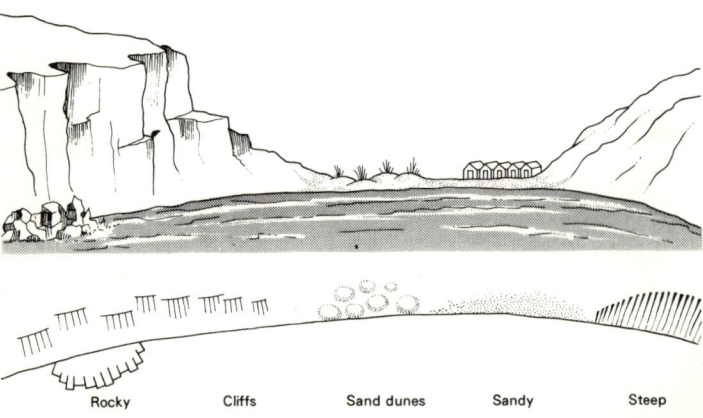

Fig.11 The coastline. Symbols used on charts.

Coastline (fig 11). Only a small amount of information is given about the landward side of the coastline: cliffs and steep coasts, sand dunes, and sandy shores are the main features.

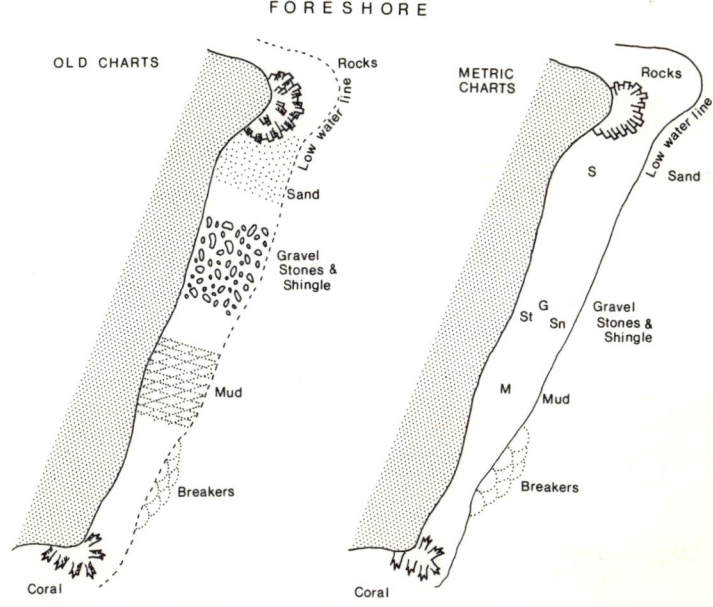

FORESHORE

Fig.12 The foreshore. Symbols used on fathoms and metric charts.

Foreshore. The foreshore is shown rather differently according to whether the chart is fathoms or metric. On metric charts the foreshore and drying areas are green, while on fathoms charts they are blue overprinted with black dots of various sorts according to the type of bottom. Metric charts describe the bottom in words or abbreviations: sand *S*, mud *M*, gravel *G*, shingle *Sn*. Rocks, coral and breakers are the same on both types of chart (fig 12).

On Land. Only those details that can easily be seen from the sea are entered on charts, such as conspicuous buildings, chimneys, churches and natural features with contour lines. Figure 13 shows a typical view when sailing down a coast with the symbols that would be found on a chart shown below it. Likewise, the approaches to a port

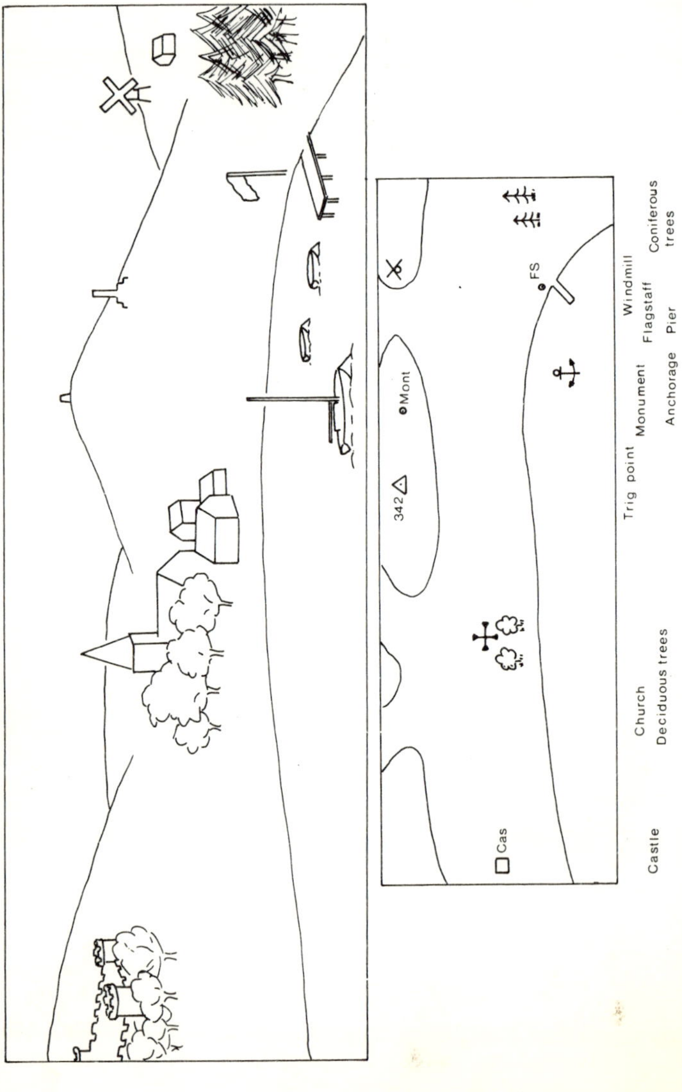

Fig.13 A typical stretch of coast showing how the objects are marked on charts.

could well look like figure 14, and the chart picks out the details which are important to ships and boats.

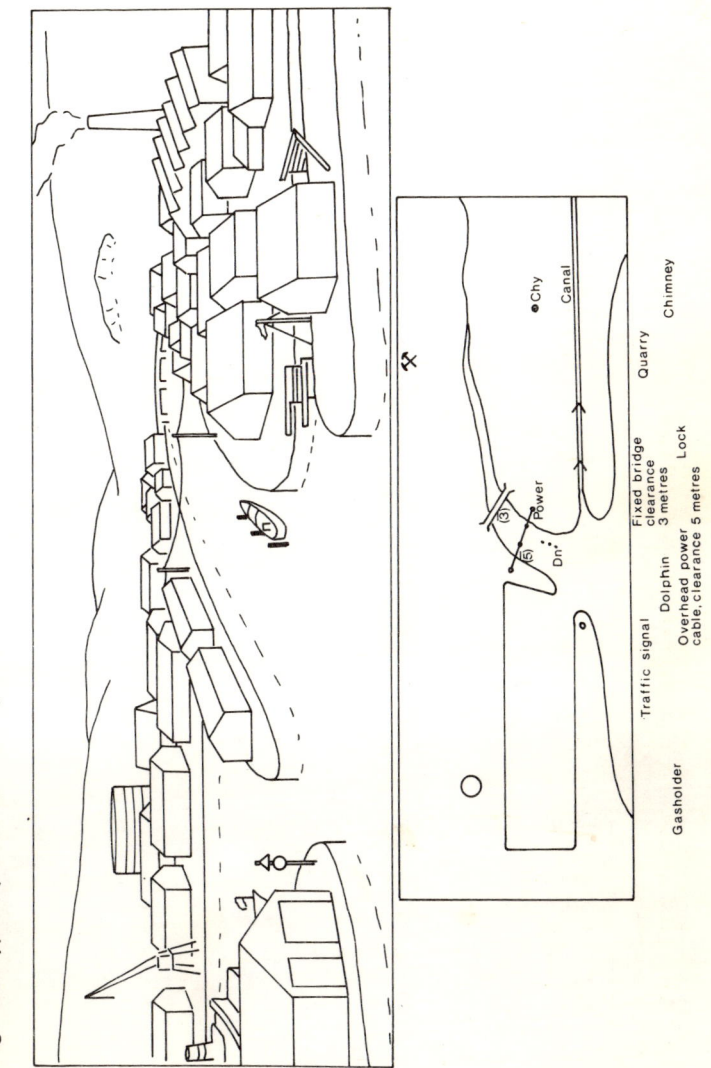

Fig.14 A typical port with chart symbols.

At Sea. Inevitably a great number of the things that are marked on charts to seaward of the low water line are submerged and therefore invisible. First and foremost come the dangers:

Dangers. The more important abbreviations are:

Bk:	bank	*Sh*:	shoal
Rf:	reef	*(PA)*:	position approximate
Le:	ledge	*Obstn*:	obstruction
cov:	covers	*Wk*:	wreck
dr:	dries	*uncov*:	uncovers

Wreck showing part of hull at level of Chart Datum

Wreck. Masts only visible

Wreck of known depth

Eddies

Tide-rips and overfalls

Figure 15. Dangers.

The sizes and positions of shoals, banks etc. are easily identified from the contour lines and the soundings:

Fathoms Charts		*Metric Charts*	
. . . . =	1 fathom line	———2——— =	2 metre line
. . . . =	2 " "	———5——— =	5 metre line
——————————— =	3 " "	———10——— =	10 metre line
--- --- --- --- --- =	6 " "		
—·—·—·—·—·—·— =	10 " "		

The Sea-bed. In Chart 5011, under the heading 'Quality of the Bottom', is a list of words used to describe the sea-bed, and their abbreviations:

Ck	Chalk	*bl*	black
Cy	Clay	*br*	brown
G	Gravel	*d*	dark
Gd	Ground	*gy*	grey
M	Mud	*lt*	light
R	Rock	*w*	white
S	Sand	*c*	coarse
Sh	Shells	*f*	fine
Sn	Shingle	*h*	hard
St	Stones	*so*	soft

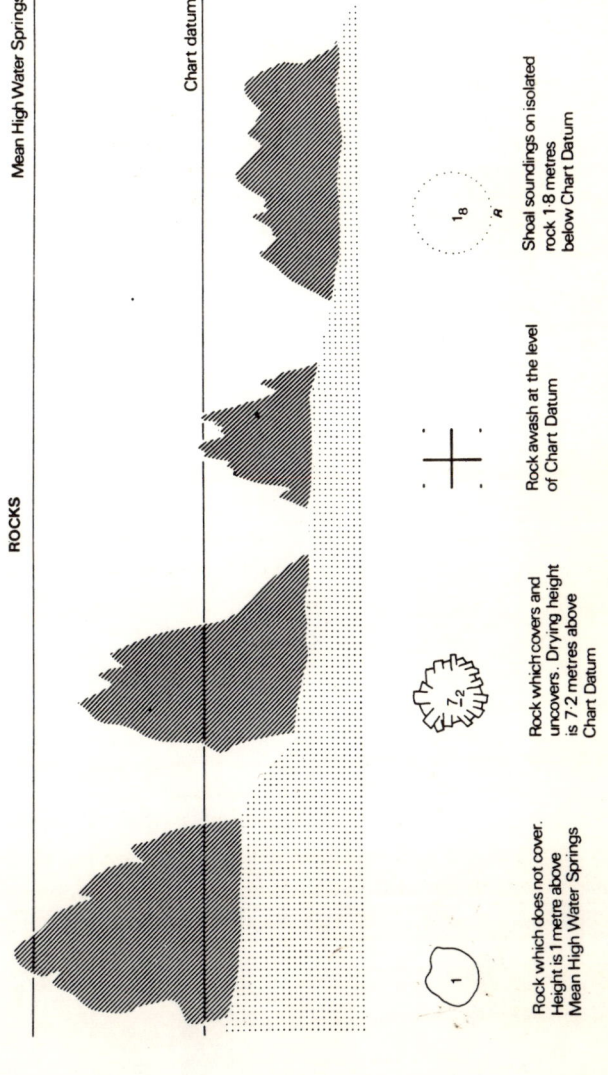

Fig. 15a Dangers, Rocks.

Rock which does not cover. Height is 1 metre above Mean High Water Springs

Rock which covers and uncovers. Drying height is 7·2 metres above Chart Datum

Rock awash at the level of Chart Datum

Shoal soundings on isolated rock 1·8 metres below Chart Datum

General Abbreviations on Charts

abt	about	*Hr*	harbour
Cas	castle	Hr	higher
Cath	cathedral	Ho	house
CG	coastguard	Ht	height
Ch	church, chapel	*kn*	knot(s)
Chy	chimney	LB	lifeboat
Cemy	cemetery	Lr	lower
cm	centimetre	m	metre(s)
Col	column	M	Sea Mile(s)
conspic	conspicuous	*min*	minute of time
Destd	destroyed	Mont	monument
Dist	distant	No	number
Dk	dock	*P*	port
dm	decimetre	*Prohibd*	prohibited
Dn	dolphin	Ru	ruins
Ft	fort	Sig Stn	signal station
ft	foot, feet	sec	second of time
FS	flagstaff	*Submd*	submerged
h	hour	Tr	tower
Hn	haven	Va	villa

Buoys and Beacons. The eye is quickly attracted by the magenta blobs on charts which mark those aids to navigation which are lit at night. The unlit buoys are less easy to pick out, but it is important to find them nonetheless, for not only do they mark a danger or a channel, but they also give the small boat sailor a good clue as to the position of his boat.

Uniform system of buoyage. This system has been agreed internationally, and many countries adopt it for marking their channels and dangers. Each country uses rather different styles of buoys which, at first sight, make them unfamiliar to anyone used to the shape of British buoys, but for the most part there is enough allegiance to the Uniform system to make them recognisable. The Uniform system is divided into two parts.

(1) *The Cardinal system.* As the name implies this is based on the cardinal points of the compass: north, east, south and west. It is not used in UK waters, but is found on the French side of the Channel. The buoys are laid to N, E, S

or W of the danger, and the colour and shape of the
topmarks tell where the danger is in relation to the buoy
(see colour plate).

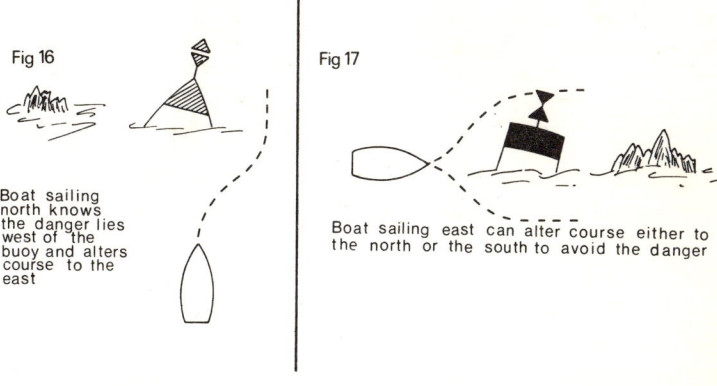

Fig 16

Boat sailing
north knows
the danger lies
west of the
buoy and alters
course to the
east

Fig 17

Boat sailing east can alter course either to
the north or the south to avoid the danger

In this way, if you are not sure of your exact position
and come across a buoy, in poor visibility for example, you
can take the right action to avoid the danger. Perhaps you
see a conical buoy with a red top and a white bottom,
surmounted by two triangles making a diamond shape; you
know that the danger lies to the west of the buoy and you
can prudently alter course to leave both buoy and danger
to the west (fig 16). Similarly the helmsman of a boat sailing
eastwards, seeing a black and white can-shaped buoy with
two triangles points together surmounting it, knows that the
danger is to the east of the buoy and can take avoiding
action by altering course either northwards of southwards
(fig 17). The Cardinal system is also used in foreign waters
for marking wrecks (see buoyage diagrams at back of
book).

(2) *The Lateral system.* This system is used for marking
channels in many countries, and is found in British waters.
Most buoys are laid for the convenience of large
commercial shipping, so the channels that are marked are
those which will be used by the larger vessels that
manoeuvre in the area.

Lateral system buoys are laid according to the direction
of the main flood, so that if you are sailing with the

flood stream you will find port hand buoys to port and, obviously, starboard hand buoys to starboard. Around the UK the main flood goes north from Land's End, round the top of Scotland and down the East coast to Dover where there is a junction with the main flood from the Scilly Isles eastwards up the Channel.

Port Hand Buoys
These are can-shaped; they are coloured red or chequered red and white (and in some countries red and yellow); topmarks when carried are also flat-topped, either can-shaped or T-shaped (see colour plate).

Starboard Hand Buoys
These are conical; black or chequered black and white (again sometimes black and yellow); topmarks are pointed, either diamond shaped or triangular point upwards.

Port	*Starboard*
Left	Right
Red	Black
Flat	Pointed

All the words to starboard are longer than the words to port which is a useful mnemonic. So too is the fact that port wine is red.

The shape of buoys is important, for it is often easier to recognise shape in poor visibility than to identify the colour of a buoy. Beware too of the effects of seagulls, for they can successfully change the colour of the tops of all buoys to white!

Where the channel is long and there are a number of buoys marking it they are often distinguished from each other by using different topmarks or no topmark on successive buoys. They are sometimes numbered, even numbers to port, and many bear individual names.

Middle Ground Buoys. There are often shoals in the middle of broad estuaries, with deep water channels to one or other side of them. Middle ground buoys are used to mark them, and they are shaped and carry topmarks so that you need only to see one buoy to identify the whereabouts of the shoal.

To differentiate them from port and starboard hand buoys they are spherical in shape and painted with horizontal stripes. Again following the direction of the main flood, if the main channel lies to starboard of a middle ground the boat will have to leave both buoy and shoal to port; it is logical, therefore, to find that the red and white horizontally striped spherical buoy at the outer end bears a flat-topped topmark: can-shaped. The inner end is also flat-topped: T-shaped.

On the other hand, if the main channel is to port and buoy and shoal are to be left to starboard, the outer end of the shoal is marked by a black and white spherical buoy bearing a pointed topmark: triangle point up. The inner end is pointed too: diamond-shaped.

If the shoal has a deep channel on both sides it is marked by red and white horizontally striped buoys, surmounted by topmarks which are neither flat nor pointed. Outer end circular, inner end a cross (see colour plate).

Light ships, Floats and Other Marks
Light vessels are painted in accordance with the Uniform system, and so are light floats which are appearing in ever-increasing size and numbers. There are also high focal plane buoys, which are much taller than the usual type so that the radar reflectors and lights which they carry can be identified at a greater distance. There are mid-channel marks, fairway marks, quarantine buoys, isolated danger marks etc. An abbreviated description of them is found on charts, and fuller details can be found in the *Admiralty List of Lights* or in *Reed's Nautical Almanac* (see colour plate).

Wrecks
Green is the colour used to mark wrecks—whether they are marked according to the Cardinal or Lateral systems—green with either a white *W* or the word *wreck* painted on them in white. All manner of buoys, light floats

B

and light vessels are used to mark wrecks, and the sailor will know where the wreck is in relation to the buoy by the shape of the buoy and the topmarks, and by looking at the chart (see colour plate).

Buoys on Charts. The symbols used on charts show the actual shape of the buoy: can, conical, spherical, spar, spindle, high focal plane, mooring and so on. The colour of the buoy is shown by means of different shading and also by an abbreviation beneath the buoy:

B	=	black	Or	=	orange
Bl	=	blue	W	=	white
G	=	green	Y	=	yellow
Gy	=	grey			

Chequered markings, horizontal and vertical stripes are all shown, and the names, numbers or letters of buoys are entered to the right of them. The symbol for a buoy covers quite a large area of water, especially on a small scale chart, so the actual position of the buoy is indicated by a small circle on the water-line (fig 18).

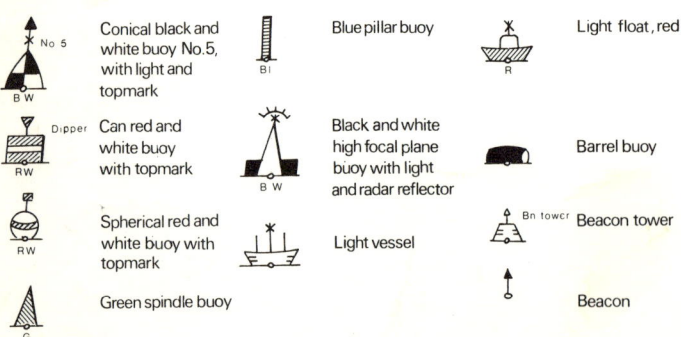

Fig.18 Symbols used on charts to depict buoyage.

The colour and shape of topmarks is shown where possible. A St. Andrew's cross on the spar above the buoy means that it exhibits a light, and there will also be a magenta splash above the symbol. A sort of spiky 'halo' is printed over those buoys that carry a radar reflector.

Beacons These are very important to small boat sailors, for they are often used to mark minor channels, small harbours and rivers etc. Many minor channels comply as best they can with the idea of the Lateral system by marking the starboard side of a channel with bare stakes, or posts with pointed topmarks, while the port side is marked with branching out withies or flat-topped topmarks. The abbreviation on charts is Bn.

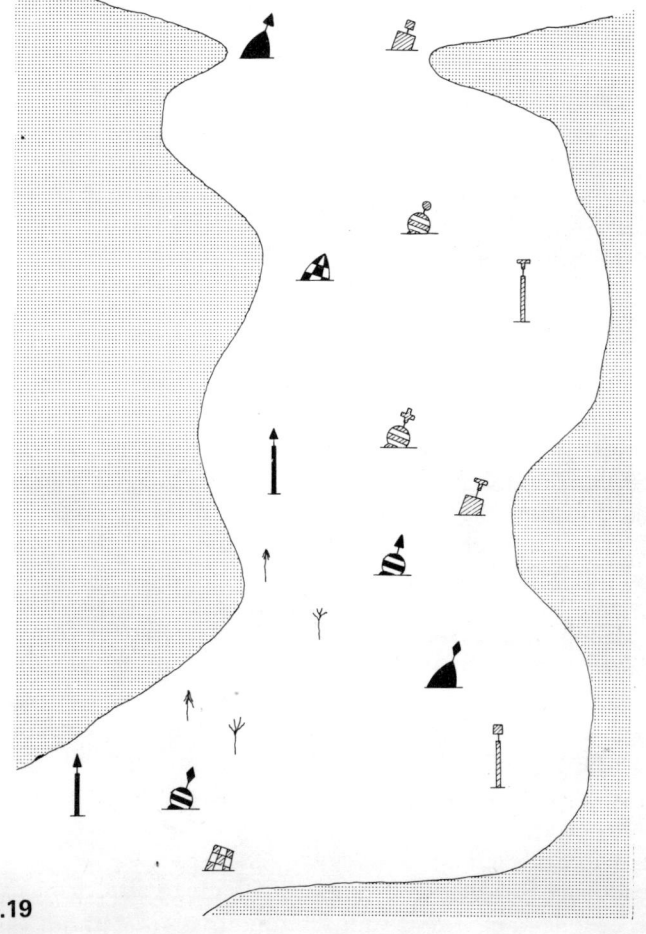

Fig.19

Test Yourself on Buoyage. Look at figure 19 and see if you can answer the following questions:

1. Which is the direction of the main flood?
2. Where are the shoals?
3. Where will you expect to find incoming and outgoing steamers?
4. Where would you choose to sail if you wanted to avoid the big 'uns?

When you have worked out the answers take a look at page 142 where there is a rough chart of the area and see if you interpreted the buoyage correctly.

Measuring Distances on Charts. Unlike Ordnance Survey maps there is no scale printed on charts. This is because a chart is distorted, as will be seen in chapter 13 where it is also fully explained why the side margins only must be used for measurements. One degree along the side margins equals 60 nautical miles, so one minute = 1 nautical mile.

Take a ruler and measure carefully the length of one minute at the top of a side margin on your chart. Compare it with the length of one minute at the bottom of the side margin. You will find that one minute at the top is longer than one minute at the bottom. On the other hand one minute at the top of the left hand margin is exactly the same as one minute at the top of the right hand margin, and you can therefore use the side margins as a scale to measure distance at the same horizontal level. *Never* use the top or bottom margins.

In figure 20, to find the distance *AB* near the top of the chart use the side border level with *AB,* and to measure the distance from *X* to *Y* near the bottom, use the side border level with *XY*. In figure 20 *AB* and *XY* are both 2.4 miles, but the figure has been drawn with a much greater increase in scale than would be found on a chart so as to make the point clear.

Practising Reading Charts. It is difficult to absorb all that you see on a chart without relating it to a stretch of water and the nearby coast—and this can be done without setting sail. Take the car and drive to various busy points along

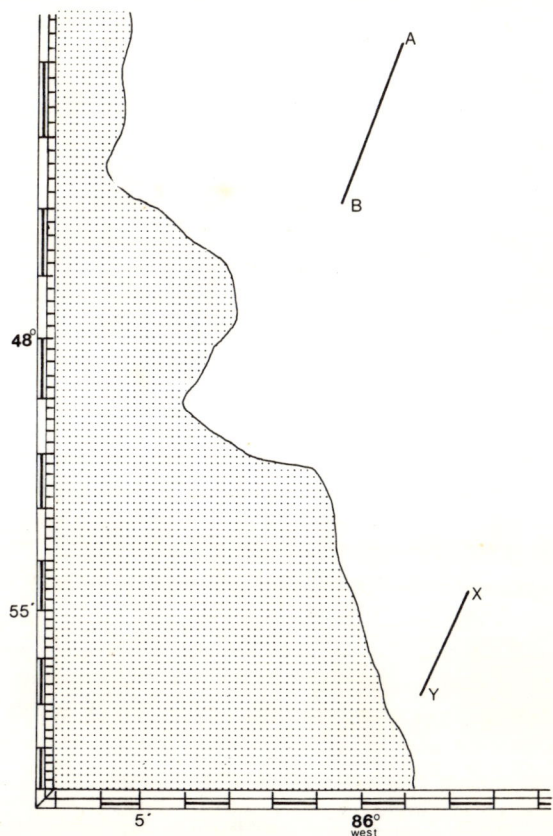

Fig.20 The scale increases higher up the chart. *AB* and *XY* are both 2.4 miles long. Check by using the side border level with the line you are measuring.

the coast, and see how many of the buoys you can spot that are marked on the chart. Look for the landmarks too, and see what channels the big ships use. A trip to a headland on a windy day will show you the position of any race that may occur off it, and a look at the foreshore at low water spring tides will reveal a number of dangers hidden at high water. You will start to gain confidence in chart reading and interpreting without the distractions of sailing your boat to interrupt your concentration.

5 : Off for a sail

By now you will be wanting to go out for a sail and put some of what you have learnt into practice. Looking at a chart when you are on dry land is one thing, but look at it when you are out on the sea, water all around you, and instead of being just a piece of paper it becomes your major link with the land.

It is a nice day; a light SE breeze is blowing and the sun is out to cheer the crew. Where shall we go? The first thing is to look up the tide tables at Appendix 1. High water for Charthaven, your nearest large port, is 0648 BST on June 2. Look up the tidal difference for the River Tee where your boat is moored. It is given in the *Admiralty Tide Tables, Reed's Nautical Almanac* or your local tide tables as + 25 minutes, so to 0648 you add 25 minutes giving you HW river Tee 0713. Low water is 1239.
Checking on the height of the water given you see that it is 5.7 metres at HW, and comparing this figure with those for the rest of the month you see that the maximum height given is 5.9 metres while the minimum is 4.8 metres. Clearly, then, it is not far off spring tides which actually occur on June 4, so you can expect to find a considerable tidal stream. With low water in the middle of the day it will be best to go out with the ebb in the morning and return well after low water when there will be a reasonable amount of water in the river.

And what of the tidal streams? Looking at the chartlets at Appendix 3 you see that they are based on HW Dover which is 09.45 BST on June 2. Enter the appropriate times on the chartlets so that you can see at a glance what the tidal stream is doing at any moment of the day. The ebb stream will be setting south everywhere on June 2 until 11.45 when it turns inshore. It has turned offshore by 12.45. It would be pointless to start the day sailing north against the ebb stream, and then later fight the flood all the way home. Obviously you will choose to benefit from the help of the south-going stream when you set out, and use the north-going flood to help you home: it should be a fast run home if the SE wind holds.

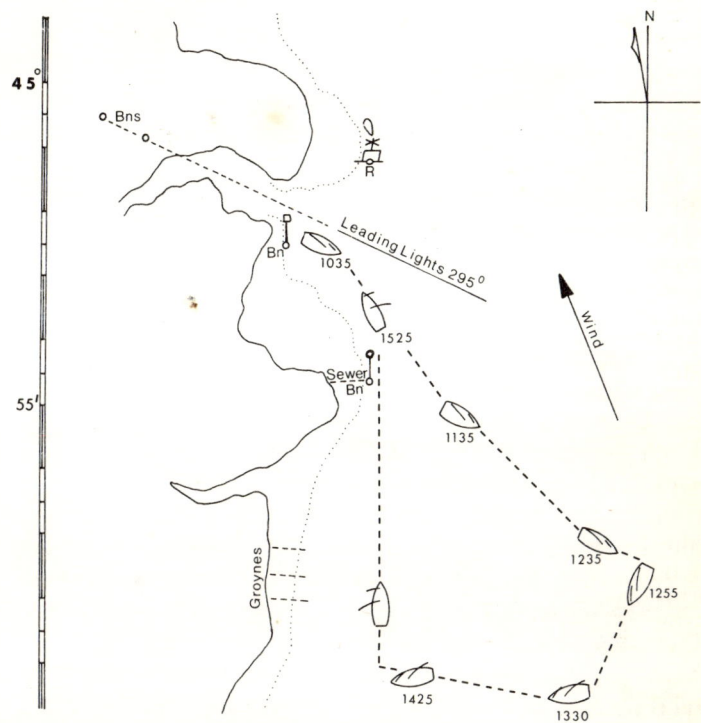

Fig.21 The boat's track on June 2.

A quick look at the chart is necessary to remind yourself of any dangers there may be. There is the buoy off the entrance to the river Tee marking the spit to the north, and beacons to the south marking the entrance and a sewer outfall; otherwise the coast is clear. Check the position of the dangers in relation to the marks.

When you are under way keep to the deep channel side of the posts or withies in the river, even when there is a lot of water inshore of them. In some places a bank may run out very gradually to a withy so that you can safely sail well inshore of it when the tide is high, but in other places the withy may mark the edge of a rocky ledge which is dangerous at all states of tide. Besides, it is ebbing, and if you run aground you will probably not succeed in getting off again for at least six hours. So keep to the channel until you have learnt from observation and experience where and what the shallows and dangers are. A look around your river or harbour at low water spring tides is never a waste of time—and you may well be horrified at some of the risks you have unwittingly taken.

Making your way down river you will have the ebb stream under you, but as you reach the entrance you will sail into the south-going ebb outside—and the change can often be very sudden. The beacon is downstream of you and the ebb will take you down on it fast, so you will probably need to bear away a little to avoid being swept on to it. Here is where good observation comes into the picture again. While you were sailing down the river you could see the tell-tale 'wake' of the ebb streaming SE past the withies, and the boats on their moorings were also swung to the SE-going ebb stream, but the beacon at the entrance shows that the stream there is setting south. There are other ways in which you can tell where the stream changes direction. You may be following another boat and see her suddenly being set sideways, or altering course and the trim of her sails to counteract the effect of the tidal stream. Alternatively you can watch the shore behind you. While you are sailing with the ebb straight down the river the shore will stay fairly steady behind you, but the moment you get into a sideways set the shore seems to slip rapidly to one side. In river Tee there are leading beacons which makes it very easy. As you sail down the middle of the river the ebb takes you directly away from them and they stay in line with each other. The moment the south-going set takes effect you will see them opening up rapidly.

So often the tendency is to look ahead, but in a boat it is very important to use your eyes all round the 360° expanse of water, and especially when you are leaving a harbour to which you are going to return. You can then make a mental note of those landmarks which will later help you to find the entrance. A good watch must also be kept for boats and ships all around you, and if you are wise you will keep clear of all of them, particularly the big ships in a main channel who do not take kindly to small yachts in their path, and may well sound a very long, loud blast of desperation which can be politely interpreted as GETOUTTERMYWAY!

Clear of all dangers at the river entrance at 10.35 you will probably decide to take a long tack out to sea on starboard, for the chartlet for 1 hour after HW Dover shows there is a stronger stream there than close inshore. The 11.45 chartlet shows that the flood starts inshore well before the main flood stream offshore.

The light breeze is from the SSE and your speed close hauled is about 2½ knots. With an occasional splash of spray flying while the wind is against the tidal stream, leave the chart in the cabin. As the boat sails out to sea the ebb sets her southward 1¾ miles in the first hour and 1 mile in the second so that although she is pointing at about 45° to the wind her course over the ground is roughly along the dotted line. During the twenty minutes from 12.35 to 12.55 it is slack water and you then decide to tack onto port. Another forty minutes close hauled brings you to a point about 9 miles from the entrance to the river. With a fair breeze and a flood you may well decide that now is the time to go and have a closer look at the shore, and a beam reach brings you about two miles from it by 14.25. The flood is well under way inshore and sets your boat to the north as you sail across it.

Visibility is excellent so you can pick out on shore all those objects that are marked on the chart and others too: the groynes, the entrance to a creek, a house, and soon you can pick out the beacons near the river. On a clear day you will find you are much further from the shore than you think, but be careful on days with poor visibility, heat haze, heavy rain or mist: the land can be much nearer than you realise, and that means that you will be sailing in shallower water than you expect. If you do bring the chart up on deck to check the objects marked on it, put it in a plastic cover to keep it dry. With the boat gybed on to starboard the coast fairly whistles past with the flood under you and you soon reach the sewer beacon. This time the set of the flood carries the boat away from the beacon at the river mouth so you can gybe and sail close past it before reaching happily up river to your mooring.

6 : Lights

The thought of being caught out at night and having to find your way home in the dark is a bit frightening for an inexperienced sailor. But when it comes to the point it is surprising how much you can see, and also how much can be learnt from the lights visible around the boat. In hazy weather it is often easier to fix the position of a boat at night, for the lights are more easily spotted than a blurred distant object in the early dawn. First a look at charts and the way that lights are marked on them.

Charts. Magenta blobs draw attention to those lights which are used for navigational purposes, and printed beside them are abbreviated descriptions of their *characteristics*. First colour—very simple:

R = red   G = green   W = white

Then the description of the light's behaviour:

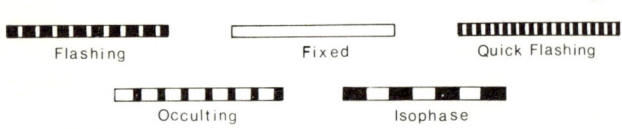

Flashing   Fixed   Quick Flashing

Occulting   Isophase

Fig.22

F = fixed. A steady continuous light. Used on shore, piers, leading lights etc.

Fl. = flashing. The flash comes at regular periods of more than a second, and the dark period is longer than the light period.

Qk.Fl. = quick flashing. Similar, but the flash comes more
    than once a second.

Occ. = occulting. Light and dark in turn, but this time the
    period of darkness is shorter than that of light.

Iso. = isophase. Periods of light and darkness are equal.

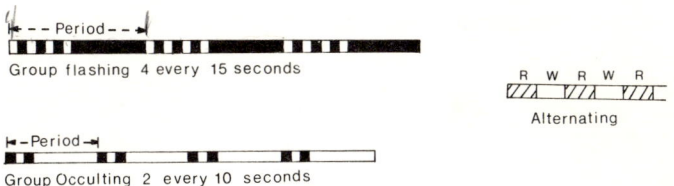

Group flashing 4 every 15 seconds

Alternating

Group Occulting 2 every 10 seconds

Fig.23

Gp.Fl. = group flash. Flashes which occur in groups
    followed by dark.

Gp.Occ. = group occulting. Occultations in groups.

F.Fl. = a fixed light which shows a brighter flash at intervals.

Alt. = alternating. A light which changes colour (*see also*
sector p. 44).

Int.Qk.Fl. = quick flashing interrupted by dark periods.

The time of a complete cycle of a group flashing or
occulting light is called the *period*—10 seconds in the
group occulting light in figure 23.

Buoys

Cardinal System. The north and west sectors exhibit white
lights, while the east and south sectors are red.

Lateral System. Port hand buoys: the red, flat-topped
marks with even numbers also have even numbers of
white flashes, or red flashes up to four.

Starboard hand buoys: the black, pointed starboard
hand buoys bear odd numbers and their lights are white
with odd numbers of flashes, 1, 3 or 5.

Middle ground buoys, middle channel buoys etc. show
lights which are selected so that they cannot be confused
with the channel markings. It is best to look each buoy up
individually.

Wrecks. Wreck buoys and light vessels are green, and so are their lights.

Lighthouses and Sector Lights. As lighthouses are built on land and therefore do not move, they give a good deal of extra information to the sailor. They are usually built as high as possible, so that the range of the light is increased. Often they mark a particularly dangerous part of the coast and many show different colours in different sectors. These are called sector lights and should not be confused with alternating lights (p43). An alternating light is seen to change colour while you look at it without changing your position, but to see the change of colour of a sector light you would have to move from one sector to another.

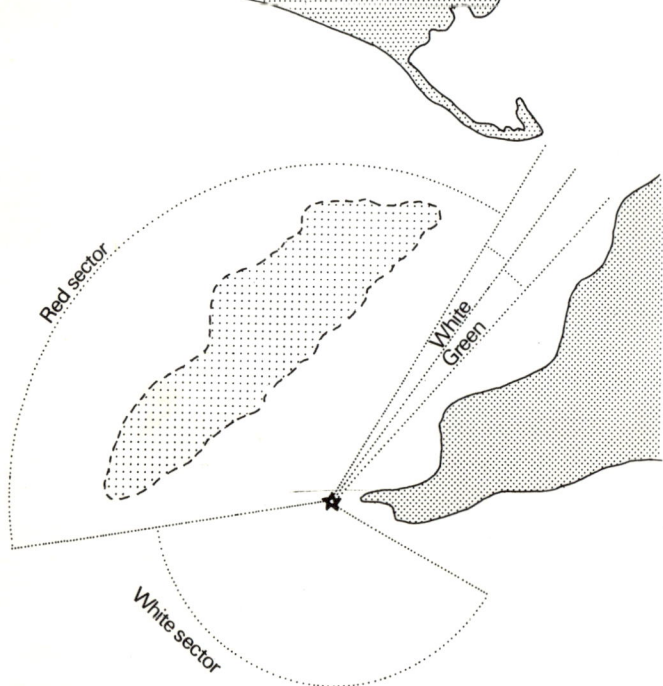

Fig.24 Needles lighthouse showing sectors.

The Needles lighthouse which is described as Gp.Occ (2) W.R.G. 20 secs, shows three colours from its main light—group occulting 2 every 20 seconds. Approaching from seaward you see a white light from 083° to 300° and know that you can sail safely towards it. If you see a red light you are too far to the north and a direct course to the lighthouse would land you on the Shingle Bank (fig 24). A ship sailing out of the Solent towards the Needles also sees a white light which leads her straight through Hurst Narrows. If she goes too far north towards the Shingles she will see the colour of the light change to red, and if she gets too close to the shore of the Isle of Wight and its off-lying dangers the colour changes to green. Sector lights are also used for marking the entrances of many ports and harbours, the River Dart and Chichester Harbour for instance.

Where to Find out About the Characteristics of Lights
a)   Charts which give the main details
b)   Admiralty *List of Lights* which gives full information
c)   *Reed's Nautical Almanac*

Lights on Vessels. The lights that a vessel must carry are laid down in the *International Regulations for Preventing Collisions at Sea.* Three basic lights must be carried by all vessels under way, whether power driven or under sail (fig. 25). These are:

Port light – *red,* showing from dead ahead to 2 points abaft the beam to port

Starboard light – *green,* showing from dead ahead to 2 points abaft the beam to starboard

Stern light – *white,* showing from 2 points abaft the beam to port, through dead astern to 2 points abaft the beam to starboard.

These are all the lights that a sailing yacht under way must carry. However, as a yacht is so close to the water and heels, lights exhibited near the deck often get masked by waves and by the sails themselves. A sailing yacht is now allowed to carry two extra lights on top of her mast, far enough apart to be clearly distinguished. The upper is red, the lower is green, and both shine over the whole of the two arcs covered by the port and starboard lights (fig 26).

Power driven vessels under way carry the basic three lights; in addition, they exhibit a white light from the foremast which also covers the same arcs as the red and green side lights. Many vessels under 150 feet carry two masthead lights, and all those over 150 feet must do so; the second is further aft and at least 15 feet higher (fig 27).

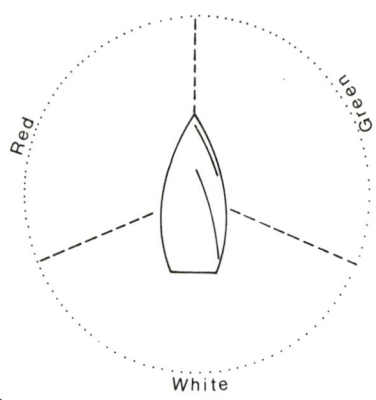

Fig.25 The basic three lights carried by vessels under way

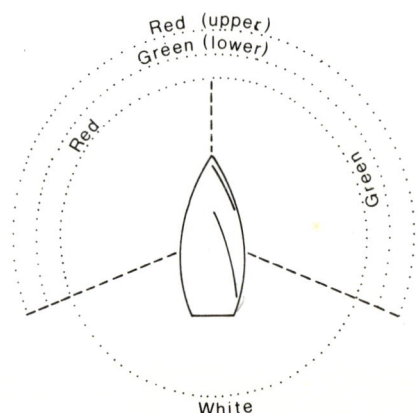

Fig.26 Extra lights that a sailing vessel may carry

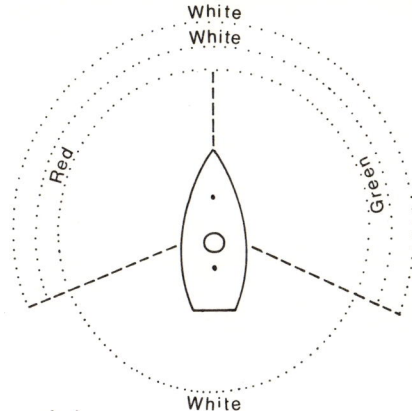

Fig.27 Lights carried
by a power driven vessel

Small rowing boats or sailing dinghies are not required to exhibit the basic three lights. An electric torch shown in good time suffices and is effective when shone onto a white sail.

Special lights. Some vessels exhibit lights to distinguish them from those which behave normally. They are visible all round the horizon and are additional to side and stern lights when the vessel is under way.

*	white	When towing or pushing, in addition to side lights, two
*	white	lights if the tow is under 600 ft. long, three lights if the
(*	white)	tow is over 600 ft. long, vertically over each other.
*	red	Vessel not under command
*	red	
*	red	
*	white	Vessel working with submarine cables or navigation
*	red	marks
*	green	Minesweeping
*	white	Pilot vessel
*	red	
*	green	Fisherman, trawling
*	white	
*	red	Fisherman, other than trawling
*	white	

If you see a boat carrying an unusual combination of lights, keep well out of her way first, and look it up in the book after you have taken avoiding action!

Anchor light. All vessels at anchor must carry a white light which is visible all round the horizon in the forward part of the boat. Should she be over 150 feet long she must also carry a white light in the stern. A boat that is aground additionally carries the two red lights above each other exhibited by a vessel not under command.

Learning to Distinguish Lights. It only needs practice to pinpoint and distinguish one light from another, and to interpret it correctly. The immediate impact on coming out of the cabin and looking at a barrage of fixed or flashing lights of several colours, near and far, is rather daunting, but it helps a great deal if you have started to learn about them with your feet on terra firma. Go to a busy channel and use your eyes—you will be surprised how quickly the lights start to make sense.

First the moving ones; they must be vessels of one sort or another. Follow the course of a steamer as she passes you and watch the side lights and masthead lights go out when the stern light comes into view.

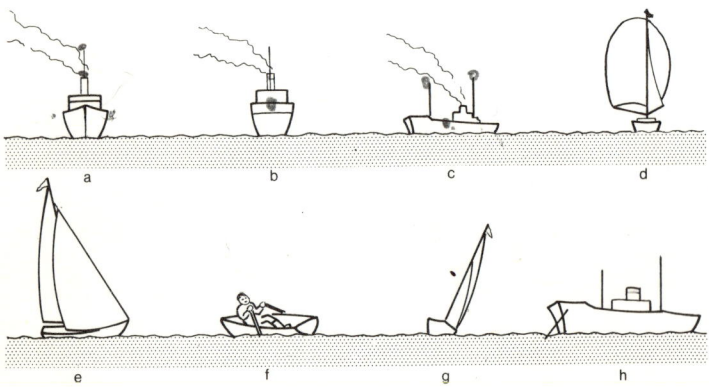

Fig. 28 Cover up figure 29 on the opposite page and try to work out what lights you would be able to see if the boats were moving or anchored like this at night.

Then look for the buoys. Unlike lights carried by vessels, lights on buoys are never fixed; they flash or are occulting. Watch them and count the seconds. Using a three syllable word between each number is a good way of pacing seconds: one bottlescrew, two bottlescrew for example. When you think you have decided what the characteristic of your buoy is, see if you can find it on the chart—and then look for another one to identify.

A bit of homework like this on shore will stand you in good stead at sea when there are other jobs that you will be doing at the same time.

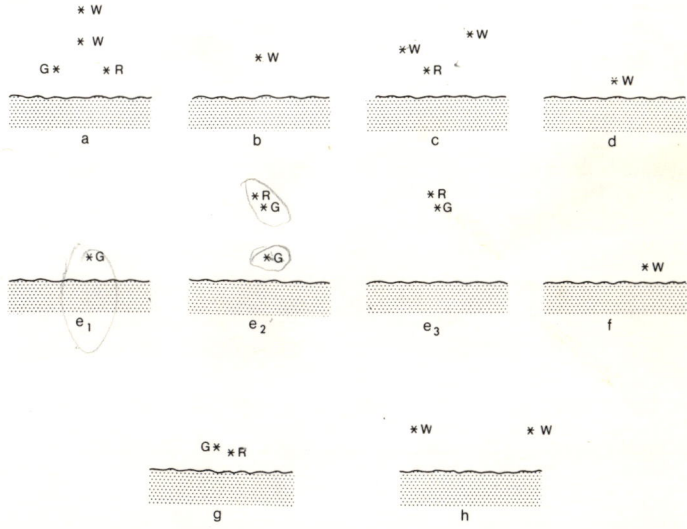

Fig. 29 Now cover up figure 28 and look at the combinations of lights above. See if you can work out what the boats are and which way they are moving.

7 : Sounding

The modern method of finding out how much water there is under a ship's keel is by means of an echo sounder. Many boats, however, rely on the age old methods of lead and line or, when racing close to a shore, on a marked pole or bamboo cane. The lead is just that, a lump of metal, hollowed at the bottom and tied on to a marked line. The hollow is so that tallow or engine grease can be put in it to bring up a sample of the bottom. This is called arming the lead and can be useful when fixing a boat's position.

If a boat is travelling fast through the water it is obviously useless to drop the lead straight over amidships for, by the time the lead reaches the bottom, the boat would be far ahead, the length of the line would be considerably greater than the depth of the water, and the skipper, thinking he was quite safe, might well sail at full speed onto the mud (fig 30). Instead the lead should be thrown far enough ahead of the boat to allow for her speed through the water; then the lead touches the bottom directly beneath the leadsman, with the line vertical in the water showing the true depth below sea level. In figure 30 the boat draws 1½ metres and the line falsely shows a depth of 9 metres. The right method in figure 31 shows the correct depth of 6 metres.

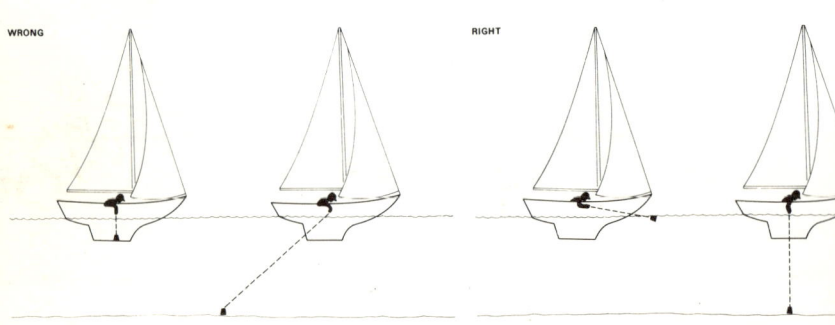

Fig.30 The wrong way to sound

Fig.31 The right way to sound. Compare the length of the line with that in figure 30.

Soundings are marked on all charts, but it is important to understand that they only give an indication of the depth of water at that point. The space taken by the printed number itself covers a fair area of sea-bed, particularly in small scale charts, and it is rare for the sea-bed to be absolutely level for more than a square metre or two. A figure of 3_4 might be printed on a chart, but the depths nearby could vary considerably. Another factor is that the contours of the sea-bed change continuously—more so in some places than in others. Winter gales often cause banks and shoals to shift, and in some places a new channel is scoured every winter, and marks have to be relaid annually. Large scale charts of much used waters obviously give much more detail than small scale ones.

As explained in chapter 4 the soundings given on charts are all related to chart datum. There are occasions when a skipper needs to know how much water there will be under his keel before reaching the spot, for example when approaching a harbour that has a bar across the entrance. Suppose that the chart shows a least depth of 1 metre, and your boat draws 2 metres. There is a slight sea running, so you want at least ½ a metre beneath your keel to allow for the fact that sea level is the half way mark between the trough and the crest of a wave. What is more, seas usually become steeper and shorter in shallow water, so it would be better to allow nearer one metre margin for safety—bumping the keel on the bottom is no fun.

First find the range of the tide by looking up the difference between HW and the preceding or succeeding LW.

	High water height	6.5 metres
less	Low water height	0.5 metres
	Range	6.0 metres.

The duration of the tide is about twelve hours so, using the 1:2:3:3:2:1 twelfths rule we know that the level of the water will rise 1/12th of the range in the first hour after LW, that is ½ metre, and 2/12ths in the second hour, 1 metre. At low water the level of water over the bar should be 0.5 metres above chart datum as shown in the tide table. So at two hours before low water and at two hours after low water the depth on the bar is predicted to be approximately:

Chart datum	1.0 metre
Height for the day	0.5 metre
First hour, 1/12th	0.5 metre
Second hour, 2/12ths	1.0 metre
Total	3.0 metres

It would be very risky to attempt to cross the bar on a falling tide after two hours before low water. When the tide is rising a few minutes' extra wait if you are in doubt is worth the delay.

There are a few occasions when the predicted height at low water is given a negative value, −0.2 for example. In this case the water is expected to fall below the level of chart datum at low water. This is pretty rare with tide tables based on LAT, but beware on such days for not only will the depths be lower but the tidal stream will be stronger. These days of major spring tides normally occur at the equinoxes in March and September, and are the

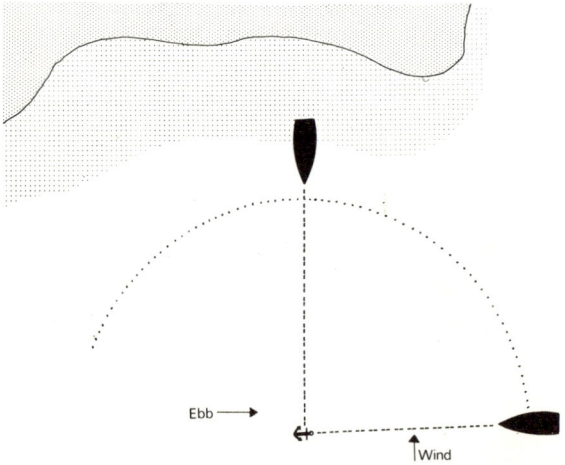

Fig.32 With an onshore wind the boat will swing at slack water and ground.

worst days of all to run aground at the top of high water.
You could find yourself waiting six months for the next
equinox before refloating!

Another occasion when you need to calculate how
much the water level will fall is when you are anchoring
close inshore. Suppose you arrive on an ebb at half tide
and want to be sure that you do not ground at low water.
With a tidal range of, say, 8 metres you realise that the
level will drop 4 metres by low water. It is not enough to
check the depth and anchor in 6 metres of water to give
you a safety margin of 2 metres. In figure 32 there is an
on shore wind and, when the tidal stream slackens, the boat
will lie to the wind at the end of a cable which is 4 metres
longer due to the fall in the water level. Be sure to anchor
far enough off shore to allow the boat to swing a full
semicircle when the flood stream takes effect.

8 : Fog

Fog—swirling damply around—is the most unnerving
experience, because so often, in a moment, a boat is thrust
into a silent world where visibility is fitful and often
virtually non-existent, where noises are distorted in
strength and direction, a sort of limbo where all the human
senses seem to be unreliable. Now is the time when a sixth
sense is needed—the sixth sense of a compass which tells
you where you are going.

If you have no compass aboard the only happy solution
is to keep such a good look-out that you are not caught
out. This does not mean just that area close to the boat,
but also keeping a regular check along the coast as far as
you can see. On a fine sunny day a gradual disappearance
of the distant coastline may be the first warning of an
impending sea-fog creeping up the shore—and it often
creeps surprisingly quickly while progress in the usual very
light winds is maddeningly slow.

It may well be that you cannot get home in time and
the fog catches you before you can pick up your mooring

and row eerily ashore. If you cannot get to a harbour in time the wisest course is to drop a hook in shallow water where deep-draught vessels cannot go. Most other vessels will be in harbour anyway. Before you drop anchor check the depth of water and the tide so as to be sure not to finish up on the mud as the level drops.

It is difficult in fog to check whether the anchor is holding properly because the shore has usually disappeared, but if you drop the lead overboard until it touches bottom you will soon see if the boat is moving over the ground. If the boat is drifting astern the lead will grow forward.

Having anchored, it is essential to keep a good watch, listening for sounds of other vessels and at the same time letting other vessels know where you are. A small boat with no compass may not carry a foghorn or a bell, but some other noise can usually be made by the crew for five seconds every minute—either by hammering a tin plate or a galvanised bucket, or by shouting if all the equipment on board is of nonresonant plastic. Naturally if the boat carries a radar reflector this should be hoisted to the top of the mast.

As has been mentioned, sounds are distorted by fog; they can seem faint when they are near and loud when they are far away. They can be reflected by the banks of fog so that they often appear to come from quite a different direction. Imagination plays tricks too—I remember swearing at a boat one night that was rushing past us far too fast in thick fog, only to find that the 'boat' was a buoy, and we were drifting past it in a flat calm on a spring flood at a good five knots.

Quite a number of buoys have fog signals and the details are marked on the charts. Bell buoys sound when the buoy rocks on the swell—and often there is no sea in foggy conditions. There are also whistle buoys, diaphons and sirens. Lighthouses, too, sound fog signals. These sounds are all from a constant direction and therefore give another clue as to whether the anchor is holding or not.

Then there are the sounds made by vessels (other than the throbbing of their engines).

A prolonged blast every 2 minutes or less means a power-driven vessel making way through the water

Two prolonged blasts means a power-driven vessel under way, but making no way through the water (i.e. not at anchor)

One blast every minute or less means a sailing vessel under way on starboard tack

Two blasts in succession every minute means a sailing vessel under way on port tack

Three blasts means a sailing vessel with the wind abaft the beam

Bell ringing for 5 seconds each minute means a vessel at anchor.

In addition, if a boat at anchor thinks that an approaching vessel may collide with her she may sound three blasts in succession, one short, one long, one short to warn of her position.

Both the *Regulations for Preventing Collisions* and common sense dictate that when visibility is poor or restricted, speed should be reduced just as is the case on the road. If engines are heard and the ship or boat is not sighted 'take early and substantial action to avoid a close quarters situation'.

9 : Position lines, transits, leading lines

Go out into your garden and stick a marker in the middle of the lawn. We will call this marker B as we are going to pretend that it is a boat surrounded by water. Standing at B look for two objects in line with each other, say an apple tree and a bird table as in figure 33. If you stand behind the apple tree and look at the bird table you will see B directly beyond it because all three are in line. Fasten a ball of string to the apple tree and unroll it past the bird table, past B and on in a straight line to the end of the lawn. Looking from the apple tree past the bird table you know that B could be anywhere along the piece of string and still be in line. Equally, wherever you put B along that piece of string it will still be in line with the bird table and the apple tree. The piece of string is a *position line*.

Now make a second position line in the same way with another piece of string, perhaps by using a fir tree and a cane in line. From B you see that both your pairs of objects are in line, the fir tree with the cane, the apple tree with the bird table. There is one place, and one place only, where this can happen—at point B. If you move a step back along the second piece of string you will see that although the fir tree and the cane are still in line, the bird table is no longer in line with the apple tree. Because the bird table is nearer to you, the apple tree will have moved back in relation to it as you stepped back: if you step forwards the apple tree will move forward of the bird table too. The exact position of B must therefore be where the

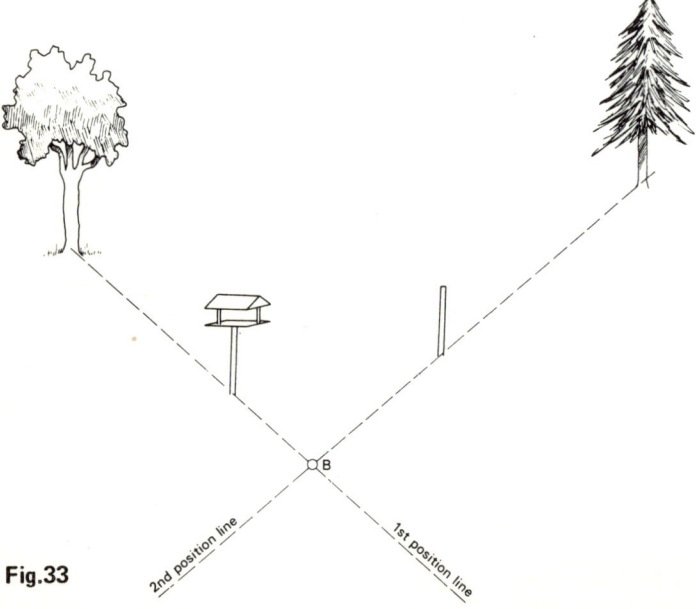

Fig.33

two position lines, that is the two pieces of string, cross each other.

Position lines are invaluable when fixing the position of a boat at sea. The moment two objects that are marked on the chart are *in transit,* that is when they come into line, you know that your boat must be somewhere along a line joining those two objects and extending seawards.

For example, when you anchor you need to know whether it is holding or not. Look for two objects on shore that are in line, and you will know that your boat is in line

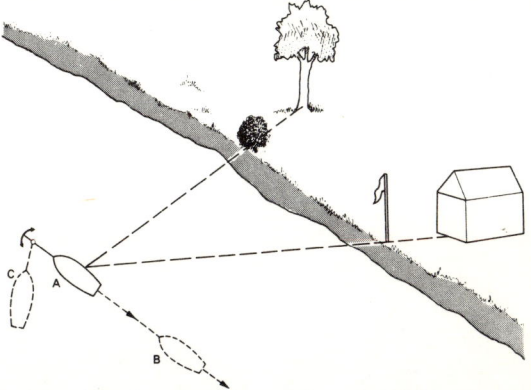

Fig.34 Anchored at *A* two separate pairs of objects are in line. If the boat drags back to *B* and beyond both pairs of objects will gradually open. If the boat swings to *C* the relationship of the two pairs of objects will change but then remain steady, showing that the anchor is not dragging.

with them. While the anchor holds the objects will stay in line, but if it drags the objects will open up, the more distant of the two moving relatively to the other in the same direction that you are dragging. We have seen on the lawn that you can move directly forwards or backwards along a position line and still keep two objects in line. It is no good, therefore, choosing two objects which are nearly dead ahead or dead astern of your boat. It is better to find two well separated pairs of objects, one of which is roughly abeam, for then you have a double check when the boat lies to a turned tidal stream or to a change in wind direction. As she swings, the objects will move out of

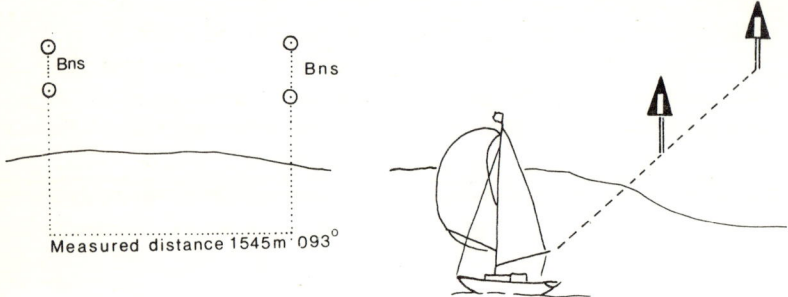

Fig.35 The markers of a measured mile in transit

line, but will thereafter stay steady in their new relationship to each other (fig 34).

Sailing along a coast you may see two posts which mark the end of a measured distance. These will also be marked on the chart, so if you draw a line from these two marks to seaward you will know that at the moment that those two marks are in transit your boat is somewhere along the line on the chart. In other words, you have plotted a position line on the chart (fig 35).

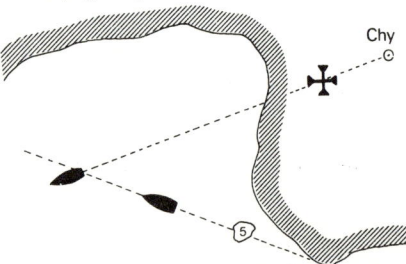

Fig.36 Sail along one transit line keeping the rock and the head in line until the church and the chimney are in line. You then know the position of your boat exactly.

The two measured distance markers were man-made, but any natural objects can be used as transits (fig 36). Perhaps a head comes into line with the top of a rock close by the shore. They are both marked on the chart so when they are in transit you can draw a line between them and to seaward, knowing that you are somewhere along it. Occasionally you can sail along, keeping one pair of objects in line until you reach the point where two other objects are in transit—and you then have fixed your position on the chart at that moment. In figure 36 you can sail along keeping the rock in line with the head until the moment when the church and chimney are in transit. Whenever you find a transit make a note of the time, and not just a mental note. If visibility deteriorates suddenly this will give you a known fact on which to work. 'One hour ago X and Y were in transit. Since then the tidal stream has been with us and added 3 knots to our speed of 2½ knots . . . so we should be about here . . .'

If you take a good look at your chart you will find all sorts of objects that you can keep an eye on, watching how they move in relation to each other, and as you get to know your home waters you will subconsciously know the approximate position of your boat at any given moment.

The question of the relation of closer objects to more distant ones is one with which we are so familiar on land that we forget about it. Driving along a road, the faster the car goes the faster the countryside passes by. If, instead of looking at objects close by, the driver looks at a far-distant hill and a house a few miles away he sees that the hill seems to move ahead of the farmhouse with the car. On land our eyes are attuned to this change in relationship, and from experience we base our estimate of speed on how quickly the relative positions of the two objects change. In a car we know whether we are going forwards or reversing, but not so at sea. The boat may be sailing forwards through the water but it often happens that an adverse tidal stream may be so strong that the boat is in fact being set backwards over the ground. A look at the shore will soon give you the answer for the boat is moving over the ground in the same direction as the more distant of two objects appears to move in relation to the nearer object.

You can use this if you are setting out to cross a tidal stream and want to sail directly to your destination. Line up two objects on the far shore—perhaps a pier and a tree.

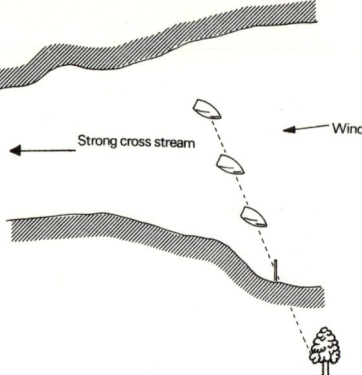

Fig.37 When crossing a strong tidal stream find two objects in line beyond your destination and sail a course that keeps the two steady.

Then sail the boat on a course which will allow you to keep those two objects in line. You will be sailing along the direct line to your destination, even if your bow is pointing well away from it (fig 37).

The same principle applies to an approaching boat. You may wonder if you are on collision courses or not. Watch the land behind her; if it stays stationary behind the boat you are on collision courses and the boat that does not have right of way must alter course. On the other hand, if the boat appears to be dropping back along the coast and you can gradually see more of it coming out ahead of her, you will pass ahead of the other boat. Should she seem to be eating up the land ahead of her, you will pass astern of her.

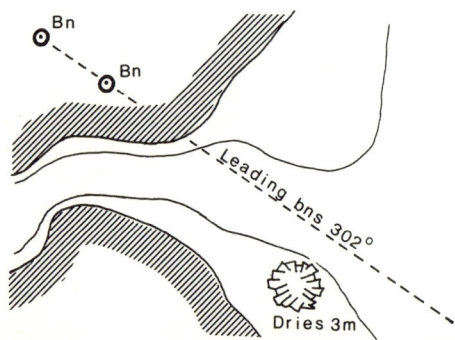

Fig.38 Leading marks

Leading marks are used in many channels to show boats the safe deep water channel. They are sited on land in such a way that when the boat sees them in line she knows that she is clear of all dangers (fig 38). As many boats sail into larger ports and harbours at night, leading marks are often lit.

When you are approaching an entrance and are looking out for the leading marks, keep well clear of the shore until you have decided quite definitely which they are. It can be disastrous to find that one of your leading marks is in fact the end of a washing line. Yes, I have done just that, and was lucky to miss the rocks which were very close by. Keep leading beacons carefully in line with each other as you sail in or out, and don't forget the effect of a strong cross tidal stream at an entrance.

10 : Introducing the compass

A small investment in a simple compass is well worth while, even for a day sailor who has no intention of going out of sight of land. The simplest form of compass used on land is the dry card compass—a magnetic needle pivoting on a pin. This is quite useless in a boat because the boat's motion causes the needle to swing so wildly that it is impossible to decide where north is.

The answer is a fluid compass. Magnets are attached to the back of a card which swings gently, damped in its gyrations by the fluid, and this card is marked on its face so that the direction to which the magnets point is labelled north. It is a magnetic compass, so it is logical to find that it points to magnetic north—of which more later in chapter 15.

The Compass Card. There are several methods of sub-dividing the card. Many are marked at degree intervals from 0° (north), through 90° (east), 180° (south) and 270° (west), and on back to north (fig 39).

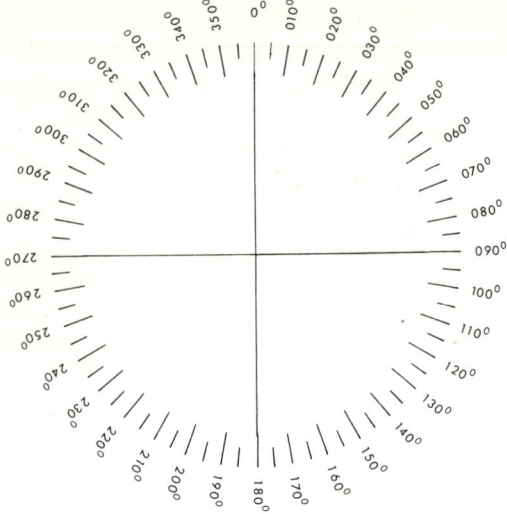

Fig.39 Compass rose marked in degrees

A second, less used method, also based on degrees, shows north and south as 0°, east and west as 90°. When using this notation directions are written: N40°E, S35°E, S42°W, N78°W.

The oldest method, and one still used regularly in sailing boats, is a card divided into 32 points as in figure 40. Each point is 11¼°, and it is often impossible to steer more accurately in a sailing boat in a seaway than to half a point or about 5°. If you are using a compass with points notation you will need to learn the points. Easiest is to remember that north and south are all-important and are always stated first whenever they occur in the name of a point. They are followed by east and west. So we have NE, SE, NW, and SW, half way between the cardinal points and next in importance. Logically, between north and north-east comes north-north-east and similarly ENE, ESE, SSE, SSW, WSW, WNW, and NNW. The names of the final 16 points start with the name of the nearest cardinal point or half-way point between them. Thus between north and west we have north, north by west, north-north-west, north-west by north, north-west, north-west by west, west-north-west, west by north, west.

Points notation is always used by weather forecasters for giving the direction of the wind, while Admiralty charts, *Pilots,* sailing instructions etc. always use degrees.

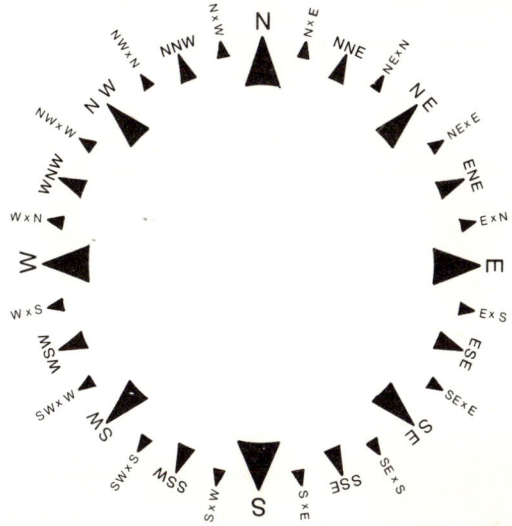

Fig.40 Compass rose, points notation

Using a Simple Compass. A little knowledge can be dangerous, but the fact remains that people often buy a boat with a fitted compass, or buy a compass and use it on board without understanding how it works and how to use the information it gives them. A compass is magnetic and points to magnetic north whereas a chart is drawn in relation to true north which is quite different. You will see compass roses on charts which look like fig 48b. The outer rose is true, the inner rose is labelled magnetic. The difference between the two is explained in chapter 15, and before relying on the accuracy of a compass that chapter should be thoroughly understood.

A relatively cheap general-purpose compass can be useful for day sailing, and the beginner can start to learn compass work and practise taking bearings provided he uses it only in conjunction with the magnetic rose on the chart and does not rely overmuch on his findings. If your boat is fitted with a steering compass which is an integral part of the fittings of the boat, and if this is what you intend to use, you will have to take deviation into account as explained in Chapter 15.

The portable compass has a card which always points to magnetic north. Although it appears that the card swings about inside the compass housing this is really the wrong way of looking at it: it is the card which stays steady and the housing which turns. You may be sailing happily in your boat, tacking from port to starboard and back again, luffing and bearing away or gybing, and it appears that the compass card is performing incredible gyrations. But stop—think again—the card is steadily pointing north, and it is you and the boat which are gyrating.

The compass is magnetic, and as is well known a magnet is attracted by certain metals, so when you are using a portable or hand-bearing compass hold it well clear of anything made of iron or steel, such as the shrouds or the engine. Otherwise the magnets will be diverted from pointing to magnetic north in the same way that a fitted steering compass is diverted.

In the housing you will see a small pointer which is fixed to the housing close to the card. This is the lubber's point. When north on the card is opposite the lubber's point the whole compass is pointing to magnetic north. When the lubber's point is opposite south-west the whole compass is pointing south-west.

For a start, let us suppose that you want to sail along a coast to *X*, but that you have seen on the chart that a shoal sticks out to seaward. Looking at the chart you can see that a line drawn from the coast guard station in figure 41 would take you clear of the danger. This line is parallel to the NW-SE line on the inner magnetic rose, and provided you keep to the south of the line you will be safe. By using your compass you can check where the coast guard station is in relation to the boat. Hold the compass at eye level, well clear of all metal, and point it directly at the coast guard hut. If the lubber's point is opposite NW on the card you will know that your boat is somewhere along the broken line. If the card reads

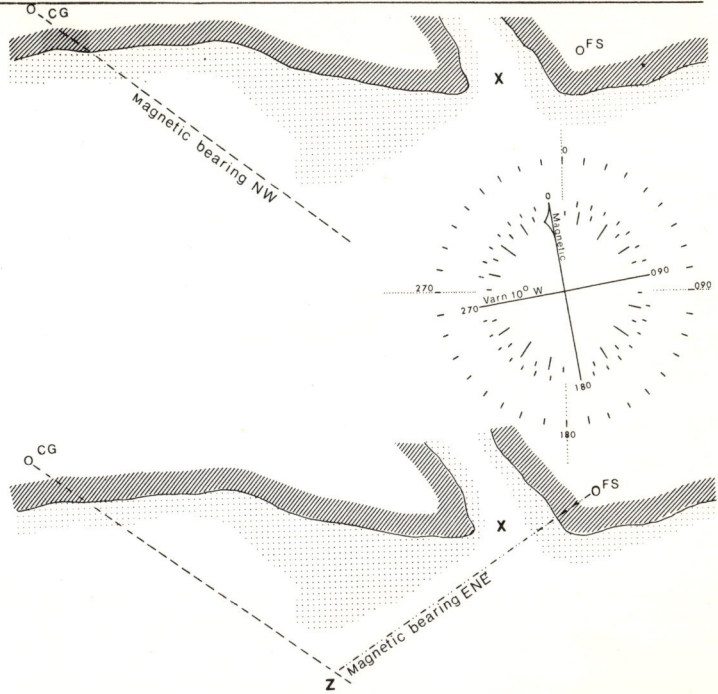

Fig.41 If the bearing of the coastguard hut is anything west of NW the boat will be to the east of the bearing marked NW and in danger of running aground. If the bearing of the flagstaff is anything north of ENE she will be safe to sail straight for the river from Z.

anything west of NW your boat is too far north and will run aground (fig. 41).

The next question will be—when can I alter course to make my way safely into the river at *X*? If I go too soon I will run aground; if I go too late I will be taking a longer route. Fortunately there is a flagstaff on the far side of the river which is also marked on the chart. In just the same way, a line drawn from the flagstaff which would lead you well clear of the shoal is parallel to the ENE—WSW axis on the magnetic rose of the chart. So use your compass to take the bearing of the flagstaff. When it bears 67½°, ENE, your boat will be somewhere along the —··—··—·· line and it will be safe to alter course for the river. There is one moment at which both the coast guard station will bear

C

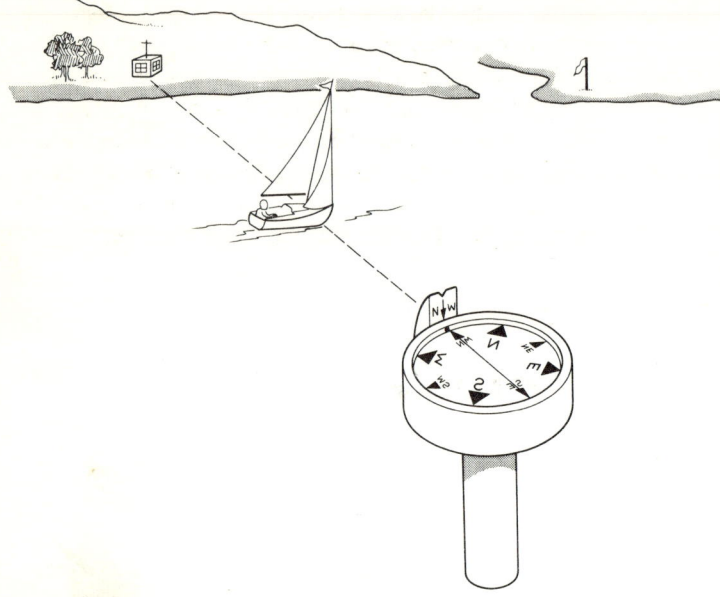

Fig.42 The bearing of the coastguard hut from the boat is NW

NW and the flagstaff will bear ENE, and at that moment your boat must be at the point where the two bearings intersect at Z.

A portable compass can also be used to decide what course a boat is sailing. In this case stand amidships and hold the compass so that the lubber's point is directly in line with the bow. The magnetic course being sailed will be that shown by the lubber's point. If your compass has a flat bottom, beware of putting it down on the engine casing when you do this—the iron will divert the compass from pointing to magnetic north and you will not be steering the course the compass indicates.

You can also use the compass to check whether you are going to collide with a ship that is to seaward of you with no land behind her. Take a bearing and repeat this at intervals. If the bearing remains the same you are on collision courses.

A word of warning. We have been using a magnetic compass and the magnetic rose printed on charts. You will see on charts that bearings are given of a number of different objects such as the leading lights 295° in figure 21. You may read in the *Pilots* or the *List of Lights* the bearings of objects or sectors of lights. These bearings are all true bearings and are *not* the same as you will take with your magnetic compass. The difference between a true bearing and a magnetic bearing is fully explained in chapter 15.

11 : A day's sailing

It is high time for another sail—this time further afield. As you will have realised, there are publications to which you will need to refer, both before and during a sail, and these should be carried on board. So far we have mentioned the following:

Charts The largest convenient scale of the area. The Admiralty also produces small but excellent Charts for Yachtsmen with sailing directions printed on the back.

Tide Tables Either the local booklet, *Reed's Nautical Almanac* or the *Admiralty Tide Tables.*

Tidal Streams Either *Reed's* or the *Admiralty Tidal Stream Atlas* for your area.

International Regulations for Preventing Collisions which can be found in *Reed's.*

To this list you should add Sailing Directions. The Admiralty prints *Pilots* for all areas, and these are full of useful information, but for day sailing you will probably find that one of the books written by yachtsmen for yachtsmen is just what you need. They usually include small port and harbour plans showing where to moor, where you can get fuel and water, where the shops are, and so on. Many print useful photographs of the coastline, some include aerial photographs which are very helpful when looked at in conjunction with charts. There is usually information about tides, tidal streams, depths of water and dangers.

Especially useful are the descriptions of approaches to ports or anchorages, for they explain clearly what to look out for, how to pick up the leading marks, and warn of problems caused by commercial or naval shipping—all written from the viewpoint of the sailor in a small boat.

Most of the phrases are easily understood, although one that is worth looking at is the expression 'keeping two objects open'. This means that you must not let them come into line with each other. It may be a rock and a headland which, if they are kept open, lead you clear of a danger. If you allow them to come into line you would be sailing into danger. 'Open three fingers' means that you should keep the two objects open so far that you see them on either side of three fingers held up at arm's length.

A list of sailing instruction publications for various waters can be found at Appendix 4.

Lastly you would be wise to take with you your own notes on the information gleaned from talking to local fishermen and fellow yachtsmen—information based on years of experience of local wind and weather and their effects on the tides and tidal streams, the changing contours of the bottom, and the hazards of man and nature alike. These notes should also include the fruits of your own experience.

So let us plan the day's sail. With a pleasant weather forecast, a morning flood and an afternoon ebb the day is just right for a swim and lunch at an anchorage 10 miles north of river Tee. If the north wind holds we should make good time on the homeward passage in the afternoon.

Never before having sailed so far north now is the time to make use of the local book of *Sailing Directions.*
There is a warning that there is a submarine cable south of the pier near the anchorage we are proposing to visit. Good holding ground is found further north, between the pier

and a line between a white boathouse on land and the
beacon marking the Madder Rocks. Lobster pots are
frequently set east of the anchorage near the rocks. There
is a useful tip about the shoal four miles north of river
Tee: the headlands north and south of the river entrance in
line lead clear of the shoal. And there is a note too about
the tidal streams. They set behind the island in a clockwise
arc on the flood and in an anti-clockwise arc on the ebb.
There is a westward set on to the Madder Rocks at the
start of the ebb.

A good look at the diagrams showing the tidal streams
and at the chart confirms these points. Yes, the line
from the two river heads does lead clear of that shoal.
There don't seem to be any other dangers likely to bother
us as the spit off the entrance to the river and the shallow
water west of the island are both buoyed (fig. 43).

What about the tides and tidal streams? On the 11th
June HW Charthaven is 14.12 BST (Appendix I) so, adding
the tidal difference of + 25 minutes, HW river Tee is
14.37; low water will be 20.30. HW Dover is 17.09.
The height given for the 11th is 4.8 metres, the lowest of
the month, so it is neaps and it doesn't matter what time
we get back to the river as we do not ground at our
mooring at neap tides. Looking at the chartlets (Appendix 2)
we see that the morning flood will help us northwards until
12.09, followed by a NE set off the Madder Rocks in the
next hour. The ebb starts inshore soon after 13.00 and is
away offshore an hour later.

A fairly early start then; sails up and a slow sail down
river against the incoming stream with a fitful northerly
breeze brings us to the entrance at 9 o'clock. A glance
astern at the leading marks shows us when we get into the
main flood stream, and we can bear away slightly to avoid
being set onto the spit to port where the buoy is heeling
well over to the north-going stream. As we pass the buoy
at 09.10, the wind settles to NNE and increases, so we
close haul on port tack to sail out into the stronger flood,
making about 2 knots.

An hour later at 10.10 it looks as though we are
somewhere about half way between the island and the

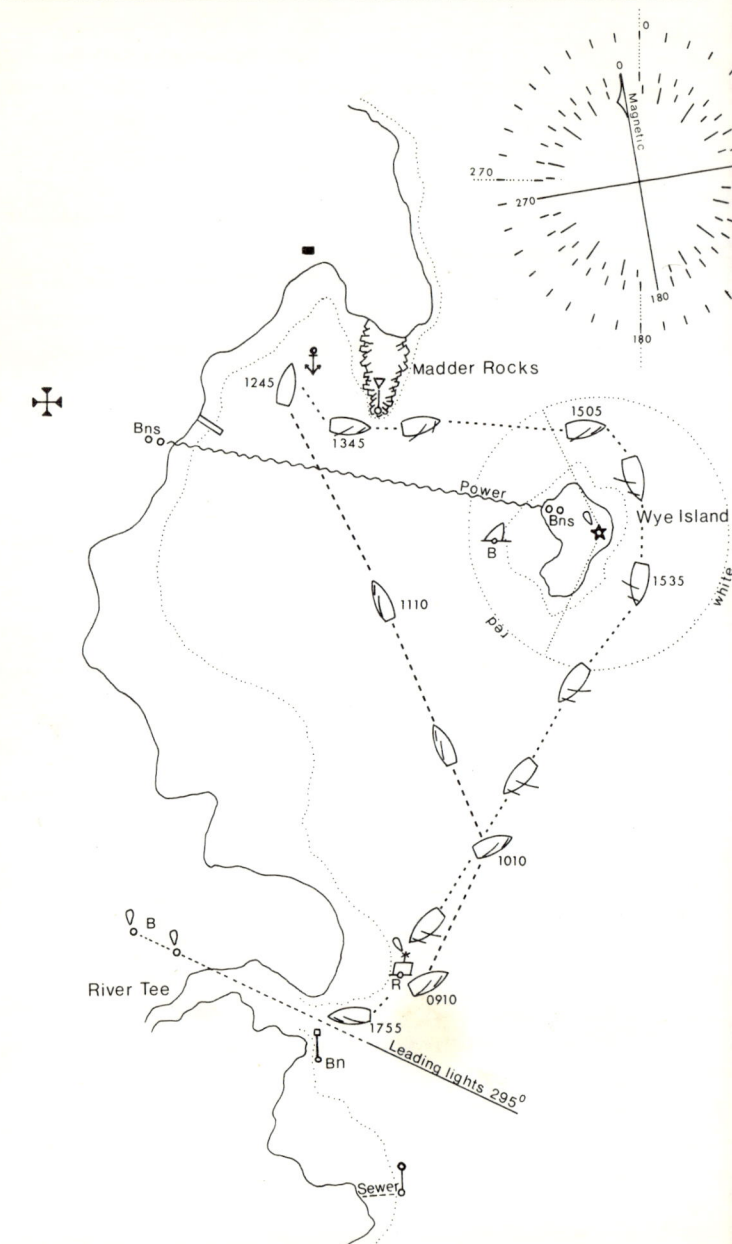

Fig.43 The boat's track on June 11.

river, and we are wondering if it is time to tack on to starboard. Where are we? The heads north and south of the river astern of us are nowhere near in line proving that we are well offshore. We can see that the lighthouse on the island is in line with the south-eastern edge of the coast so we have one position line. A bearing would fix our position and there is a chimney on the shore which is also marked on the chart. Standing up and holding the portable compass well clear of all distracting metal influences such as shrouds, engine and pushpit, we find that the chimney bears roughly WNW magnetic. Using the inner magnetic rose on the chart we can draw a line WNW-ESE from the chimney, and this line crosses our position line on the lighthouse at a point about 4 miles from the island. If we tack now, the tidal stream will help us on our way and we shall be heading towards our anchorage. The breeze is increasing slightly, and our speed with it to about 3 knots.

An hour later, at 11.10, the bearing on the chimney has changed to slightly south of west, the buoy marking the shallows west of Island Wye is just forward of the beam, and both river heads are still visible. We are heading rather above the pier and are well over half way, nicely placed for an approach to our anchorage. The clockwise set shown on the chartlet during the next hour will be easing all the time, but will help by setting us to windward. As we sail closer to the shore the wind eases slightly in the lee of the land, and our speed drops a little. At 12.45 we are far enough inshore to drop anchor, well clear of the submarine cable, and find that she lies quietly head to wind in almost slack water.

As we are going to land and eat our lunch ashore it is even more important to be sure that the anchor is holding, so we recheck our two pairs of markers ashore before getting into the dinghy. After landing we must also find a mark on the opposite shore in line with the boat so that we can check that the anchor is holding while we are on land.

Back aboard after lunch we decide to return via the outside of Island Wye—the wind has backed to north, light here in the lee of the land but nearer moderate offshore judging from some small boats sailing out there. The sea is benign, the day is gorgeous—it would be a pity to rush home and cut the sail short. Setting off at 13.35 we note that the boat is now lying to an ebb, and we remember the warning that at the start of the ebb there is a westerly set on to the Madder Rocks. There is a very convenient transit that we have found on the chart. The shore end of the pier and the spire of a church about 2½ miles inland give us a good line south of the Madder Rocks and north of Wye Island. This will be a big help for it is often very difficult to decide how much a boat is being set by the tide when sailing seaward if the coast you are leaving is featureless. How often does one swim out from the shore only to be astonished when turning back to find how far one has been set away from a pile of clothes. Swimming back home is easier because one can see the clothes and the cliffs or dunes behind them, and swim a crab-like course towards them. So when sailing seaward check how much you are being set by keeping an eye on the shore astern.

Once past the rocks, and keeping an eye open for those lobster pots, it will be as well to sail rather above the direct line of the pier and the church, firstly because the south-setting ebb will be increasing, and secondly in case the wind lightens or veers again. We shall then have a little in hand to seaward of the island. Running rapidly down the eastern side of the island we pass the lighthouse at full speed at 15.20 with the ebb under us, and soon sight the river. Knowing that the ebb will be setting us south we will need to point above the river entrance until we can spot the buoy marking the spit at the entrance. Once we have found it we can line it up with something on the shore behind—ah yes, that clump of trees. If we hold the trees in line with the buoy we shall sail directly to it, and then be able to pick up the leading marks in the river.

We would have no problems if it were night. We could sail along the line where the white sector of the lighthouse on Wye Island changes to red until reaching the buoy, and then sail up the middle of the channel using the leading lights.

Observation. Whether it is your first sail, your hundred and first, or your thousand and first, you will always learn

something new—if you keep your eyes open. Winds and
tidal streams are never constant, and however well you
think you know your waters you will continually be
surprised. Therein lies much of the joy of sailing. So
remind yourself of what you observed during your sail.

The Tidal Streams. Did the stream turn earlier inshore than
in the middle of the channel? Mostly you were sailing far
from the shore, but there were other boats closer in. By
comparing their performance with your own you could
make your own estimate of the set and rate of the stream
inshore.

Did you find an unexpected set somewhere? If so make
a note of it—it could be useful if you are battling against
an adverse stream one day.

Did you see any patches of turbulent water and local
eddies to avoid in heavy weather? Their position may well
change according to whether the tidal stream is flooding or
ebbing.

The Wind. After all, the wind is a sailing boat's engine.
Without wind she cannot sail, with too much she is wet
and uncomfortable. What influence did the coast have on
the wind? It was lighter in the lee of the land, and
probably more variable in direction, especially when
affected by clumps of trees on shore. If you had been
sailing close under some cliffs with the wind from the
shore you would probably have found that it struck the
boat at a downward angle, causing her to heel a lot in the
gusts. And what was the wind doing in the distance? The
chimney was useful, showing what the wind was doing on
land. Perhaps the smoke showed a different slant ashore,
perhaps it was climbing straight up, showing calm.
And what of the other sailing boats around? Did they have
the same wind as you, or did you see them becalmed
somewhere, or enjoying quite a different breeze?

Did you spot any changes in good time so that you
could make use of them?

The Shore. Did you make a note of any useful landmarks

and transits for the future when you may need to know exactly where you are?

And did you check that all the buildings marked on the chart are still standing, and note any new ones?

Fog. Although it was a lovely day, did you keep a check on the distant coast to make sure that there was no impending fog or bad visibility?

Other vessels. Did you see any commercial traffic and note the track taken? Were there any large vessels at anchor so that you could check the set of the tidal stream there? Were there any fishing boats or dredgers around which could be expected to be in much the same area on future occasions?

Navigation marks. You checked your position against the various buoys and beacons but did you remember to think what they meant to the large vessels around? When you were close enough to see the lights, did you check them on the chart, and practise identifying their characteristics?

Estimating. If you were wise you practised estimating:

1. how fast your boat was sailing through the water
2. how much leeway she was making
3. the set and rate of the tidal stream
4. how fast your boat was sailing over the ground

These are all factors which you will need to use in future when navigating accurately, both in and out of sight of land.

Cautions. Did you take care to anchor clear of submarine cables, foul ground etc? It is expensive to lose an anchor, but it is very unpopular to cut the electricity supply or the telephone lines. Did you check whether there were firing ranges and other prohibited areas to avoid? These are marked on charts for your own safety so that you can keep away from them.

Did you avoid those areas where there is a lot of commercial traffic, and particularly areas where big ships manoeuvre with difficulty?

You did, of course, check whether your chart was metric or marked in fathoms?

At the end of a day's sail. Think back critically and decide how you could have done better and how you have earned a pat on the back. Would you have been able to get home safely if the wind had dropped entirely? Did you have lights on board in case you couldn't get back in daylight? And what if a thick fog had enshrouded you? Did you have a foghorn on board or some means of letting other boats know your position? Or suppose a thunderstorm had blown up. Would you have been clear of danger, or could you have been set on to some rocks or the shore?

Summary. The contents of the foregoing chapters are well within the capabilities of every yachtsman. They should be known, understood and used when day sailing around the coasts. Practice brings familiarity and, like regular use of the rear mirror when driving, observation and interpretation become a subconscious habit. The foundation of navigation is use of charts, tides, tidal streams plus observation.

All that remains now is for you to apply the finishing touches which are presented in the chapters which follow. If you have absorbed and practised what you have read so far you will be surprised at how little, in fact, needs to be added.

12 : Navigational equipment needed for coastal cruising

As soon as a boat owner decides to start real cruising he must get down to learning how to navigate accurately. Approximations can be dangerous, and the sea does not tolerate the man who relies on guesswork and good luck. The more he has practised using his charts, his compass and his eyes, the easier it will be to learn.

The equipment needed is as follows:
Charts, both small scale and large scale (see chapter 13) pencils, rubber, clean dividers that open and close easily but which are not loose, a magnifying glass for small print and either a parallel ruler or a protractor.
Sailing Directions.
Nautical Almanac, supplemented where necessary by List of Lights, Fog Signals, Tide Tables, Tidal Stream Atlas.
Log book.
Steering compass and hand bearing compass (see chapter 14).
Log or speed indicator.
Lead or echo sounder.
Radio
Barometer and chronometer.
These are the essential items of equipment. In addition, many boats carry direction finding equipment of some sort and an increasing number of boats are now equipped with radar.

(1) *Sailing Directions.* As well as the books written for the yachtsman listed at Appendix 4 there are sailing directions published by the Admiralty covering most parts of the world. Those covering the more frequented home waters are:

  27 Channel Pilot
  28 Dover Strait Pilot
  37 West Coast of England Pilot
  40 Irish Coast Pilot

53 North Sea Vol II (East coast of Scotland)
54 North Sea Vol III (East coast of England)
66 West coast of Scotland Pilot

The *Pilots* list the charts published by the Admiralty for the area and give general notes on fisheries, pilotage, traffic, tidal streams and tides, coastguard, storm signals, buoyage systems, meteorological and natural conditions etc. The coast is then described in detail, accompanied by drawings and photographs from seaward. Headings in this, the main part of the *Pilot*, include anchorages, buoyage, dangers, obstructions, races, eddies, piers, lights, fog signals, coastguard, submarine cables, channels, foul ground, bye-laws, facilities, landing places and direction and rate of tidal streams. There are no wasted words in the *Pilots* and, used with charts, they build up a detailed picture of any part of the coast.

(2) *Nautical Almanac.* A good nautical almanac is a must on board a cruising boat, and is probably the most thumbed publication in her library. *Brown's* and *Reed's* are both excellent and appear annually. *Reed's* is angled more towards the small boat sailor, while *Brown's* is more for those with a professional interest and wider horizons. Tide tables, tidal stream chartlets, chart symbols, radio beacons, buoyage systems, collision regulations, tables for celestial navigation and a list of buoys and lights in home and nearby waters are only the main items. There is much else besides.

(3) *Tide Tables, Tidal Stream Atlases, Lights, Fog Signals, Radio Signals, Times of Meteorological Forecasts.* Home waters are thoroughly covered in *Reed's,* and so are some nearby foreign waters, but when a boat is going foreign she will need to carry information in detail about the waters she is going to visit. The Netherlands Hydrographic authorities, for example, publish an excellent atlas showing the tidal streams around their complex shores.

(4) *Buoyage Systems.* Most buoyage conforms to the Cardinal and Lateral systems which are printed in the

Admiralty Pilots and *Reed's* (see colour plate)
There are, however, some countries such as the
Scandinavian countries which use different systems, so it is
always wise to check before sailing into their waters.

(5) *Log Book.* As well as a log book in which to keep a
permanent record of a voyage it is best to have a rough
note book for use when spray is flying and drips make
their way into the cabin. In this you can enter details of
your course, distance sailed, position, bearings, barometer
readings etc. to which you will refer later. The information
can later be transferred to your permanent log book.

(6) *Log and Speed Indicator.* It is even more necessary to
know how far the boat has sailed when out of sight of land
than when you can check your progress against the
changing coast line. It is often quite difficult to gauge the
speed of a boat through the water, particularly when the
winds are light and variable. The well-tried method is to
stream a log and line. A spinner turns at the end of the line
which is hooked to a register fastened to the stern. As the
boat sails through the water the spinner and line rotate,
turning the mechanism of the register. The dial records the
distance sailed, and some also record the speed.
  When manoeuvring in shallow water the helmsman must
remember that as the boat loses way, perhaps when going
about, the spinner sinks to the bottom and could be lost if
it fouls an obstruction on the sea-bed. Similarly, crossing
close ahead of another boat could cause the same trouble
if she sails over it and cuts the line. Another problem is
due to the rotation of the spinner which puts so many
turns into the line that if you try to coil it as you haul in
the spinner you end up with a magnificent cat's cradle!
Instead, unhook the line from the register and pay it out
astern as you pull in the spinner. The sea will straighten
out the kinks, and you can then coil the line neatly,
starting at the spinner end.
  Instead of towing a log which inevitably slightly reduces
the speed of a boat through the water, racing yachts and
other boats too may carry a speed indicator which usually

records both the speed of the boat and also the distance
sailed through the water.

(7) *Lead and Echo Sounder.* The use of the lead has
already been described in chapter 7. Remember that the
deeper the water, the further ahead of the boat the lead
needs to be thrown to give it time to sink to the bottom
before the leadsman is vertically over it.

Echo sounders are a modern alternative and well worth
the cost. An impulse travels from the boat to the bottom
of the sea and back again. The time taken is measured and
converted to a figure which gives the depth at that spot.
This is read on a dial.

(8) *Radio.* Weather forecasts are of enormous importance
to small boat skippers and often prevent a boat being
caught out in a gale. Times of British and foreign forecasts
should be noted before starting a cruise.

(9) *Barometer and Chronometer.* Small boats are at the
mercy of the weather, and every hint about approaching
conditions is invaluable. Forecasts are frequently right, but
the actual timing of, say, a vigorous depression can be
hours out. The barometer and observation of the clouds
can be of great help here. *Reed's* gives useful hints, and a
book of meteorology aboard makes interesting reading.
Always note the barometer reading in your log, for it is the
change in pressure that is important when forecasting.

Time enters into so many facets of navigation that a
good ship's clock or chronometer should be carried. The
best of watches can get smashed or dropped overboard,
whereas a chronometer fastened to a bulkhead is much less
vulnerable.

(10) *Direction finding equipment and Radio aids.* Many
yachts nowadays carry D/F equipment, and there are
skippers who rely on navigating by radio virtually to the
exclusion of normal coastal navigation procedure. This is a
mistake. D/F is invaluable as an *additional* means of fixing
a boat's position.

Radio beacons emit signals and, just as a hand-bearing compass is used to take bearings of a visible object, so D/F equipment is used to take bearings of an audible radio signal from a beacon marked on a chart. Every beacon has its individual signal, and a number of beacons all broadcast in succession on the same frequency so that a boat can obtain a fix by taking a bearing on two or three of them. For example, on 291.9 kc/s the following beacons transmit in succession:

Portland Bill	PB	· —— ·	— · · ·	
St. Catherine's	CP	— · — ·	· —— ·	
Cap d'Antifer	TI	—	· ·	
Le Havre	LH	· — · ·	· · · ·	
Pointe de Ver	ER	· · — · ·	· — ·	(è, not e)
Pointe de Barfleur	FG	· · — ·	— — ·	

To rely on radio signals alone is unwise. A station may cease transmitting at the crucial moment while it is being repaired or serviced, or the boat's D/F equipment may break down. Sky-wave effect causes errors at night when the beacon is more than 25 miles away, and there can be errors due to your boat and your crew. It is important, therefore, always to carry on with routine dead reckoning procedure as described in chapter 18. *Reed's* has an extremely useful chapter on the use and problems of D/F, and also explains the Loran, Decca and Consol radio ship position finding systems.

Chart facing page 81
Reproduced from BA chart No. 262C with the sanction of the Controller, HM Stationery Office and of the Hydrographer of the Navy.

Chart facing page 80
Reproduced from BA Chart 'New Symbols and Colours on Metric Charts' with the sanction of the Controller, HM Stationery Office and of the Hydrographer of the Navy.

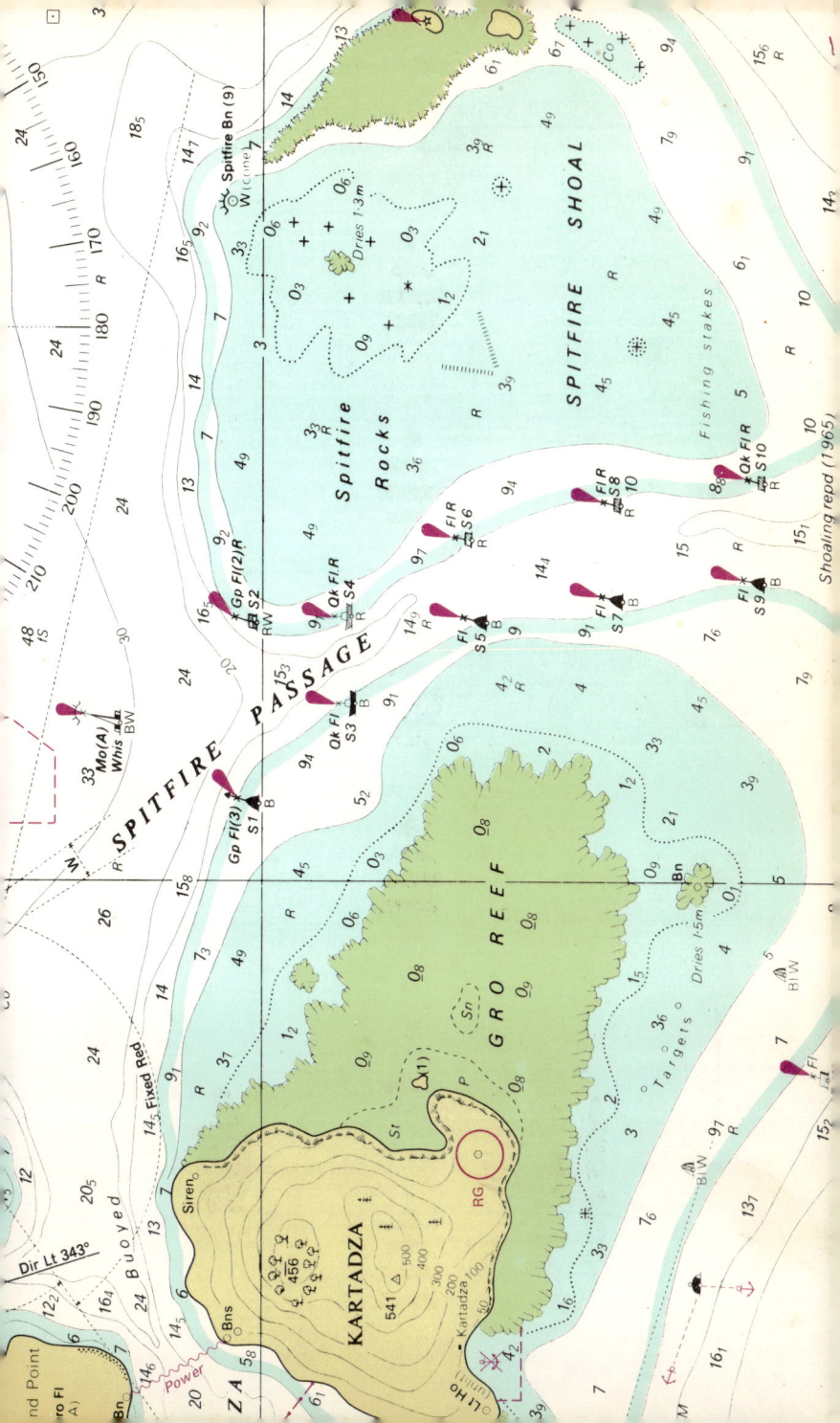

LATERAL SYSTEM
MIDDLE GROUND
Channels of equal importance

PORT HAND
MARKS

STARBOARD
HAND MARKS

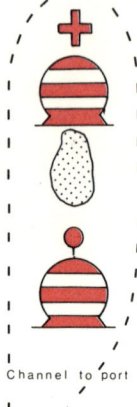

Channel to port

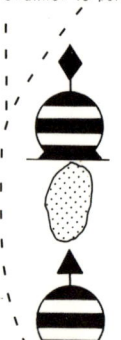

Channel to starboard

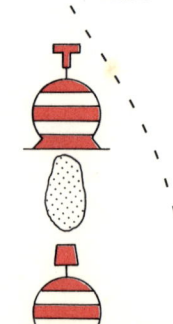

Direction of main flood

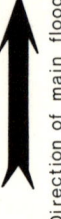

CARDINAL SYSTEM

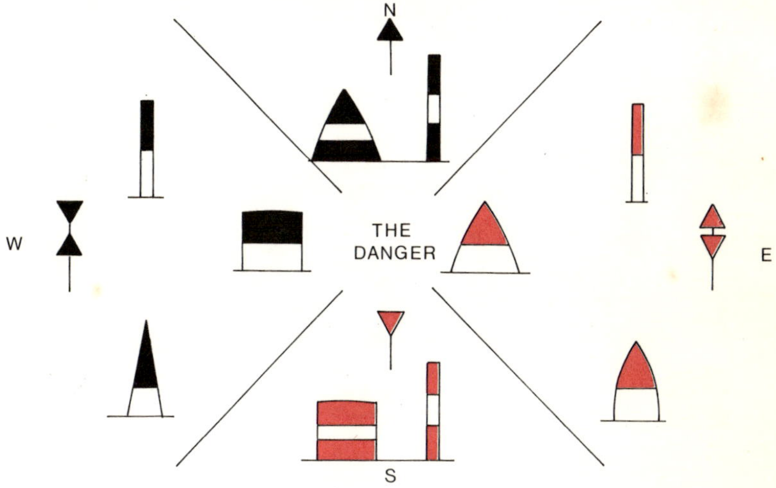

N

THE DANGER

W

E

S

Cardinal system

WRECKS

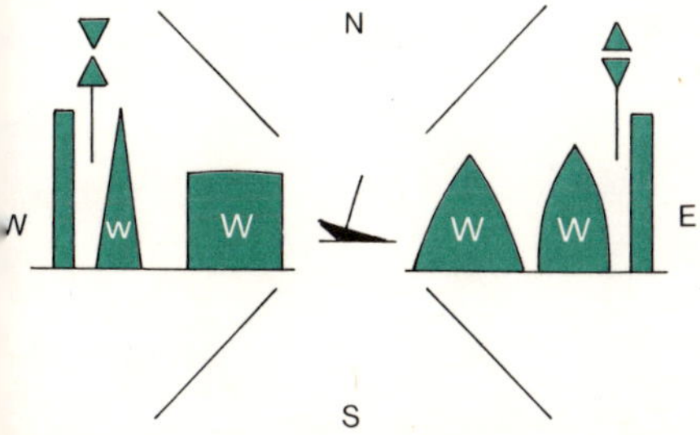

Lateral system

N

W

E

S

Leave to port

Leave either side

Leave to starboard

OTHER MARKS

Mid-channel marks

Transition marks

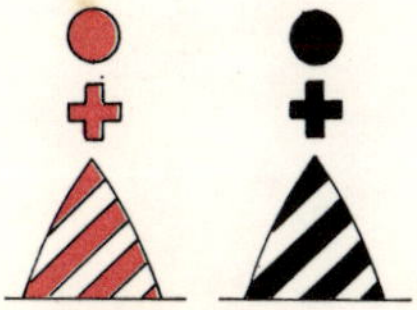

Fairway marks

Quarantine

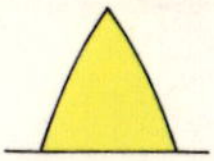

Isolated danger

Outfall

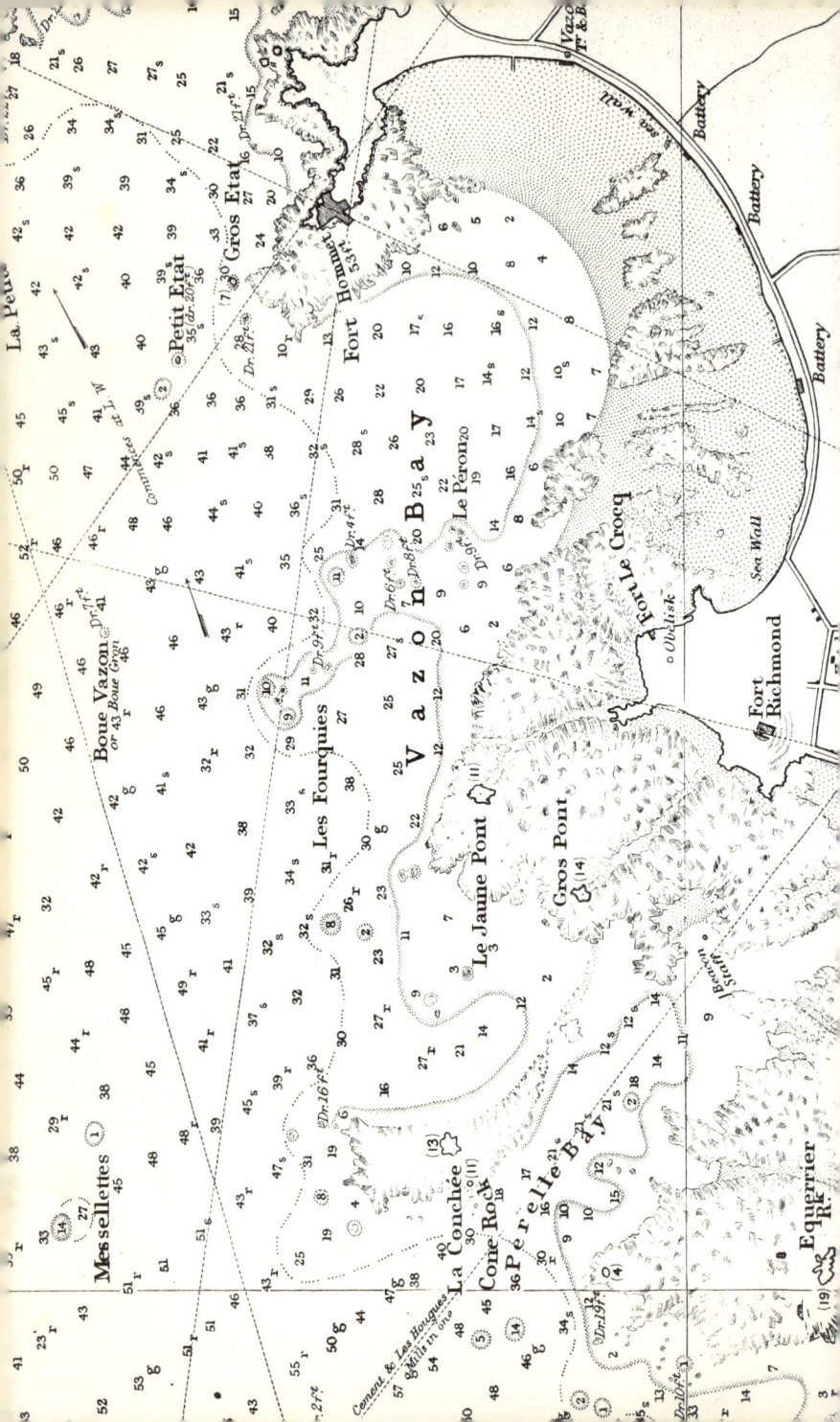

13 : Charts again

A full set of charts should be carried, covering all the waters that a boat is likely to sail in, and that includes those areas into which she may be forced by heavy weather. Charts must be of various scales to cover the navigator's needs, for it is no use trying to enter a harbour using a chart which covers the whole of the British Isles.

Small scale charts will be needed for the main part of a longish passage, medium scale charts for details of the coasts at departure and arrival points and any tricky areas en route, plus large scale plans of the ports themselves if they are not adequately covered in your book of sailing instructions. Thus for a trip from Portsmouth to St. Malo you need small scale charts of the Channel—and that means coverage well to eastward and westward of the direct route. Medium scale charts should cover the British coasts, the Solent, the Channel Islands generally and the French coast. Rather larger scale charts of the East Solent, Alderney, Guernsey, Jersey and the approaches to St. Malo are advisable in these tricky waters. Should the weather deteriorate you may decide to nip into a convenient port for shelter so you will either need large scale plans of likely ports or the relevant books listed at Appendix 4. The area covered should be westward at least as far as Portland and Lézardrieux, and eastward to Le Havre and Beachy Head.

Apart from Admiralty charts there are a number of excellent publications by the Hydrographic Departments of foreign countries, and these can be used satisfactorily as the symbols are internationally agreed. So, if on arriving at some foreign port you decide to visit an unexpected area before returning home, you can safely buy foreign charts knowing that you will be able to read them. Always study the information under the title, and in particular confirm the level of chart datum and the units used for soundings.

If a chart is to be relied upon it must be up to date. The Admiralty issues weekly Notices to Mariners, listing any changes that have been made. Under the left hand bottom border a note is made of all small corrections, giving the year and number of the relevant Notice. Charts should be kept up to date by entering corrections as Notices are issued, but few yachtsmen are so thorough. At least take charts to an Admiralty agent for correction at the beginning of each season and before going on a long cruise. All corrections must be made in waterproof ink.

Taking Care of Charts Never use ink or indelible pencil. Use a soft pencil and you will then be able to erase the lines you have drawn using a clean soft rubber, and your chart will be ready for your next voyage. Fold charts as little as possible and stow them flat. When you are working on them with a parallel ruler or protractor any bump caused by an unnecessary fold is a great nuisance and makes accurate work difficult.

Charts must be kept dry; if you are wearing a sou'wester and come below on a wet night, as you bend over your chart the drips will pour off and soak it, making it impossible to draw pencil lines on it. Try too to resist the temptation of taking the chart on deck to compare it with the coast. The chart can get soused by an unexpected wave—or worse. Passing Start Point one windy night I announced 'We don't need that chart any more', and at that moment a gust of wind whisked it out of my hands and overboard! So, keep charts below decks, flat and dry: you need them.

Latitude, Longitude and Position First a quick look at our nearly round earth and the gridwork of lines we superimpose so that we can describe exactly where any particular place is. The earth rotates around an axis, at one end of which is the north pole, at the other the south pole. Half way between them, around the circumference at its broadest, runs the equator. At right angles to the equator meridians run north and south to the poles. Lines of latitude are drawn parallel to the equator (fig 44).

Lines of longitude, the meridians, are marked in degrees, minutes and seconds east and west of $0°$, the meridian of Greenwich, up to $180°$. Lines of latitude are similarly

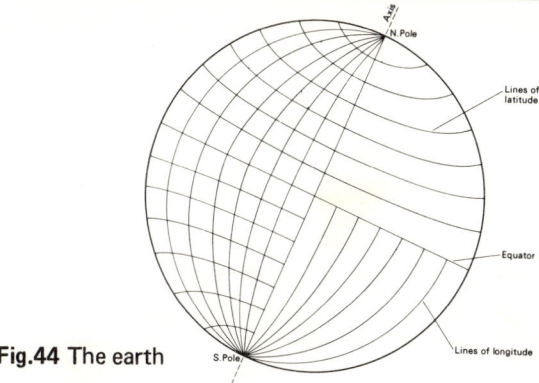

Fig.44 The earth

marked from 0°, the equator, to 90°N, the north pole, and 90°S, the south pole. Any particular position on the surface of the earth can be pinpointed, lying as it does at the junction of a meridian and a line of latitude. For example:

45° 32′15″N   38°04′53″ S
                or
10°18′34″ E   12°19′00″ W

Distance. The distance between any two degrees of latitude is the same all round the earth. It is 60 sea miles from 3°S to 4°S whether you are sailing near Borneo, off Ecuador or on Lake Victoria. Longitude is a very different matter for the meridians all converge at the two poles. If you sail from 5°W to 6°W at the equator south of Ghana you cover 60 nautical miles. North of the Faroes 5°W−6°W is only about 30 miles, and by the time you reach the North Pole the distance between them has shrunk to nil.

Mercator Projection. A chart is a flat piece of paper, whereas the surface of the earth represented on it is not flat but curved. The chart therefore has to be drawn in such a way that the navigator can use it to take accurate measurements of distance, and so that he can find the correct course to steer to make his way from one place to another.

The characteristic of Mercator charts—and most

Admiralty charts that the small boat sailor uses are drawn
on Mercator projection—is that lines of longitude, the
meridians, are drawn parallel to each other and at right
angles to the lines of latitude. Inevitably the surface of the
earth is distorted as portrayed.

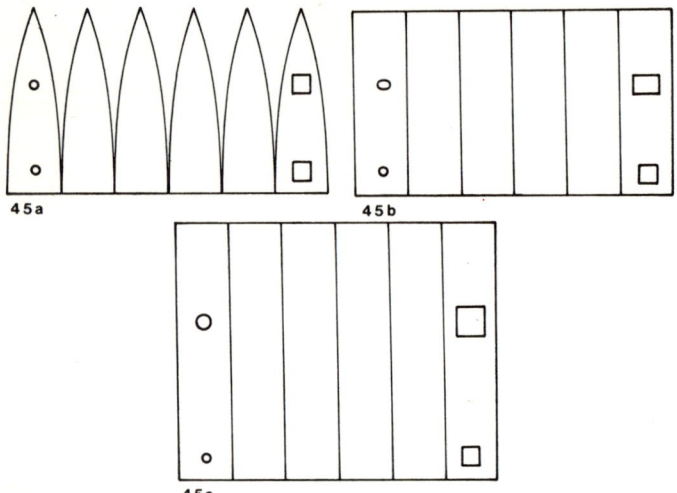

Fig.45a Half an orange cut into segments from the pole to the
equator and flattened.

Fig.45b Stretching the peel so that the cuts are parallel to each other
and at right angles to the equator causes distortion and the upper
square becomes a rectangle.

Fig.45c Stretching the peel upwards in the same proportion as it is
stretched sideways causes the scale to increase from bottom to top,
but keeps the shape of objects near the top in proportion. The
square at the top is much larger than the square at the bottom,
but encloses the same area of land.

How a chart is made can probably best be understood by
using an orange, which is much the same shape as the
world. Cutting it in half we will use the 'Northern
Hemisphere' only—having enjoyed the fruit! Cut the peel
down from the 'pole' along a number of 'meridians' at
right angles to the 'equator'. If you now flatten the peel so
that the equator is as near as possible a straight line you
will find that you have a series of nearly triangular shapes,

separated at the top and meeting at the equator (fig 45a).
You want those meridians to run parallel to each other and
at right angles to the equator with no gaps in between,
which is what they do on a Mercator chart. The peel has
therefore to be stretched sideways—only a little near the
equator, but a great deal near the pole. The result is that a
square drawn on the peel near the top of a segment is
stretched sideways so much that it becomes a rectangle (fig
45b). Latitude and longitude are quite out of proportion,
and the old lady that so many people see in Britain's
coastline becomes a gross misshapen dwarf.

To avoid this disproportion a Mercator chart is stretched
upwards as well as sideways, so that the length and breadth
of land at the top remain in proportion to each other. The
scale therefore varies. On the orange the square at the
bottom in figure 45c really encloses the same area of land
as the square at the top; it is only the way that the orange
has been stretched that makes the top area appear very
much larger. This is why Greenland appears to be larger
than Africa on Mercator maps of the world, although in
reality it is less than half the size. Gnomonic projection is
used for areas near the poles—unlikely to be visited by
yachtsmen—and also for large scale harbour plans.

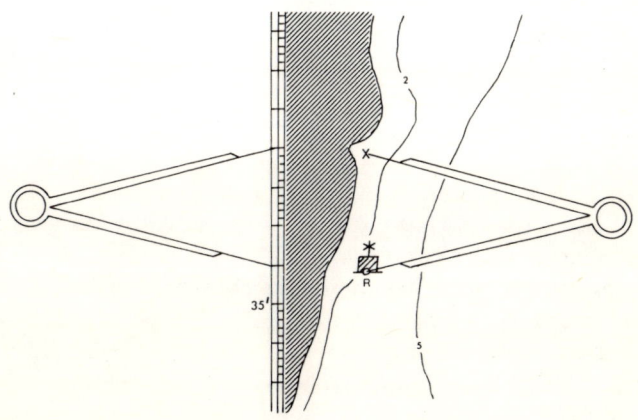

Fig.46 Distances must be measured along the side borders at the
same level.

Measuring Distances We have already noted that the actual distance between two degrees of longitude varies from 60 miles to nil, so it is clearly no use trying to use as a scale the degrees of longitude marked on the top and bottom borders. On the other hand we know that the distance between degrees of latitude remains constant, and that one minute of latitude = one nautical mile. So to measure distance we stretch our dividers between X and the buoy in figure 46 and find the distance between them using the side border at the same latitude. At the same latitude? Why? Because the scale, as we have just found, increases from bottom to top but remains constant from left to right.

14 : More about the compass

The Steering Compass Perhaps your boat is already fitted with a steering compass. On the other hand you may only decide to buy one after sailing her for some while. There are important points to bear in mind.

(1) *A Compass must be easy to read when you are at the helm.* Boats vary so much in detail that you alone can decide on the best place. Some boats have their compass high on a bulkhead where it is read at eye level, some instal it further aft where the helmsman looks down at it. Best is to go and look at as many other boats as you can and see what their arrangements are, and also what type of compass they use. A chat with the skippers will soon give you an idea as to both the advantages and disadvantages of their lay-outs and whether they have chosen the right place and right type of compass.

Some compasses are designed to be read horizontally, and these should be installed fairly high up, while a compass that you need to look down at should be placed relatively low. Some people prefer a grid compass, and they do have their advantages.

Easy to read: bear in mind long hours at the helm and choose a clear card which you can see easily, even when spray is flying, and especially if you wear spectacles which become salt-encrusted. Much cruising is done at night, and the compass must be properly lit, brightly enough to read without strain, but not too bright because of interference with night vision.

(2) *A compass must swing freely.* Whatever type of compass you choose it must be able to swing in all directions without knocking against part of the boat. It must be properly gimballed, otherwise the card will not be

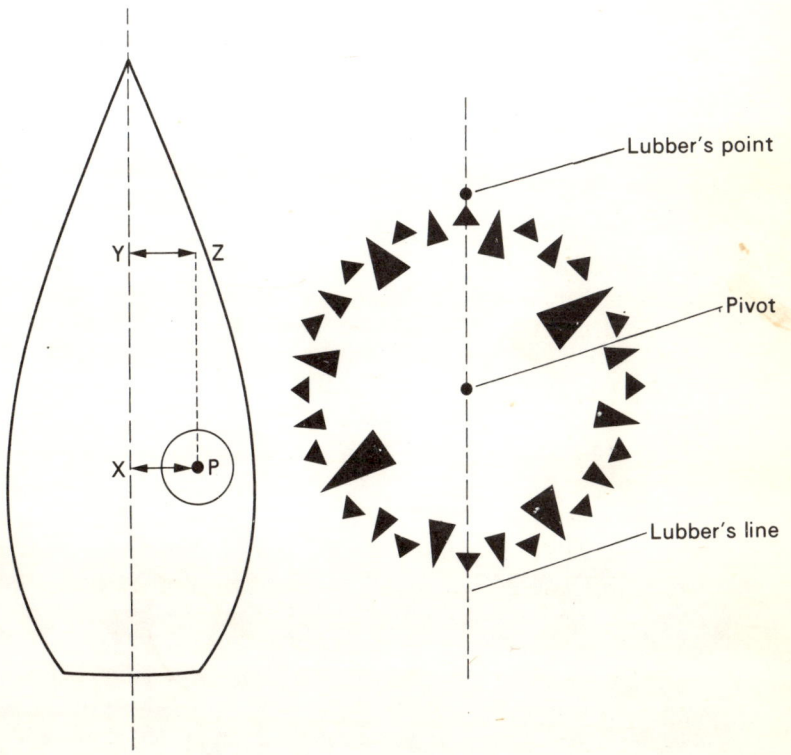

Fig.47 *X* to the pivot point *P,* and *Y* to *Z* are equal. Hold a marker vertically at *Z* and sight along the line Pivot–lubber's point–*Z*.

able to move freely and you will not be able to steer a
proper course when the sea is high and the motion
considerable.

(3) *A compass must be sited so that the lubber's line is
parallel to the fore-and-aft line of the boat* (fig 47). The
lubber's line is the imaginary line between the lubber's
point and the point around which the compass card pivots.
When the helmsman checks what course he is steering he
looks at the lubber's point and reads his course on the card
adjacent to it. To him the lubber's point represents the
bow of the boat, and this can only be true if the lubber's
line is parallel to the fore-and-aft line of the boat. Suppose
that an error was made and the compass installed grossly
out of parallel some 10° to the fore-and-aft line. The
helmsman, blithely steering due east according to his
compass, would be 10° off course. If your compass is
installed amidships you can check by sighting along it, and
if it is OK you will see the pivot point, the lubber's point
and the bow of the boat all in line. If the compass is to one
side of amidships you will need to measure how far and
then hold a boathook, batten or flagstaff vertically near
the bows the same distance from amidships. If the compass
is properly installed you will see the pivot, lubber's point
and your boathook are all in line.

(4) *Deviation.* A compass is magnetic, and is therefore
influenced by all iron or steel aboard a boat which pulls
the card away from pointing to magnetic north. The
amount by which the compass is diverted from magnetic
north is called deviation, and as all boats have varying
amounts of metal aboard, sited differently in relation to
the compass, deviation varies from boat to boat.
     Unfortunately the iron and steel aboard, and indeed the
hull itself if the boat is made of steel, set up a magnetic
field which influences the compass differently according to
which course the boat is steering. It is therefore necessary
to discover the degree of deviation for a number of
different courses. This is done by swinging ship, and
although it is advisable to have a skilled man for the job

for a start, it can and should be checked by the skipper and crew. Basically the idea is to check the compass reading against a known and accurate bearing: the difference between the two is the amount of deviation. In a small boat it is easiest to moor fore-and-aft, and then swing her round gradually, finding the amount of deviation for each of 16 points of the compass. You can then write out a deviation table for use when plotting (see Appendix 3).

The compass is often found to deviate by a considerable amount, and may need to be corrected. This is definitely a job for an expert who will reduce the deviation figure by means of permanent magnetic correctors. These must not be moved after they have been fixed. He will also deal with heeling error which is caused by the change in the relative vertical position of the engine or an iron keel and the compass above them when a boat heels.

Once the boat has been swung, and any necessary correction made, care must be taken to make no alteration to the disposition of metal objects in the boat. If a new engine is installed the boat must be reswung, corrected if necessary, and a new deviation table drawn up. Equally, if a member of the crew stows a frying pan just forward of the compass on the far side of a bulkhead, or leaves a spanner close by, the compass will be affected, the figure you have painstakingly established for deviation will no longer apply and you will not be sailing the course you have plotted.

Hand-bearing Compass. You will need to take accurate bearings when you start cruising seriously. Sometimes a steering compass is fitted so that you can also use it for taking bearings. More often, however, a hand-bearing compass is used, and there are several types available. Whatever type you choose the system is to line up the object on which you are taking a bearing with the sights of the compass and the lubber's point or black line in the bowl. Sounds easy? Try it in a big sea! This is a knack which comes only with practice, and the important thing is to chock the lower part of your body well so that you can move the upper part freely, acting as a human gimbal as you counteract the motion of the boat, keeping eye and compass steady, vertical and pointing at your object. Don't forget to keep well away from *all* metal influences so that your bearing is not affected: lifelines, shrouds, pushpit, pulpit, the steering compass itself, the engine—luckily the gold fillings in your teeth will not affect it! They would be difficult to remove.

Whenever an opportunity arises, test your skill against a transit and see how accurate you are. You can also use bearings printed on charts, but these are given true so will need to be corrected to magnetic if you are to compare them with your bearing taken with the hand-bearing compass. The next chapter explains how to do this.

Taking Bearings with the Steering Compass. You can use the steering compass to take bearings by lining the whole boat up with the object and finding the course. This is really a two-man job. The helmsman positions himself amidships so that he is in the fore-and-aft line, and when he sees the chosen object directly over the bow he shouts. The second member of the crew reads the compass bearing. Two or three shouts are advisable—it isn't as easy as it sounds, especially in anything of a sea. Because the bearing has been taken with the steering compass it will be subject to deviation and must be corrected before being entered on the chart.

15 : True—magnetic—compass

A certain number of parallels of latitude and longitude are printed on all charts, and if you look at the compass roses you will see that these parallels are drawn N—S and E—W in relation to the outer of the two roses. This, the true rose, points to true north, the North Pole itself. The inner rose, the magnetic rose, points to magnetic north which is rather to one side of the North Pole (fig 48b). Wherever you are, you are on two meridians: the true meridian

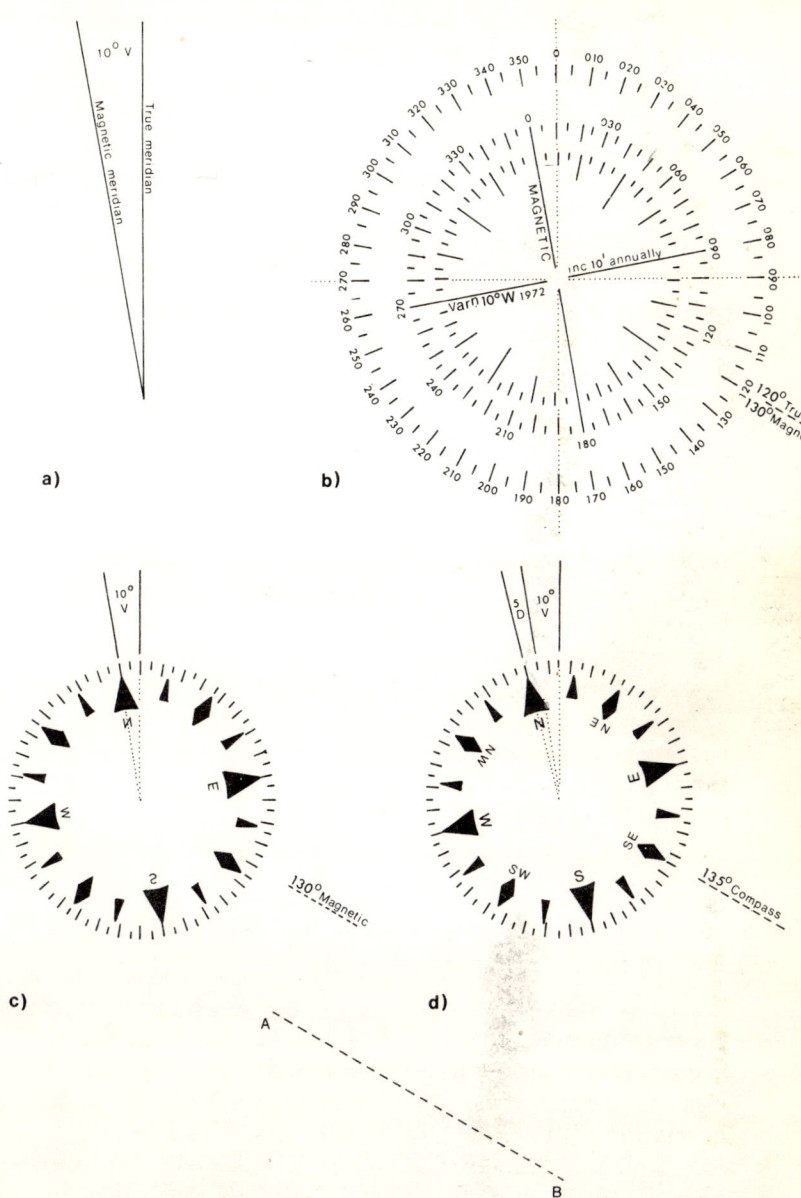

Fig.48 *AB* can be expressed in three different ways: 120° True, 130° Magnetic and 135° Compass. Variation is 10°W, deviation is 5°W.

which extends from the south pole, through your position, to the north pole, and the magnetic meridian which extends similarly to the magnetic north pole (fig 48a). The angle between the true and the magnetic meridian is called variation—and it is well named. Not only does it vary in different places but it also varies from year to year because the magnetic pole wanders.

Details of variation are printed on the W—E axis of the inner magnetic rose: e.g. 'Varn 11°30 W (1970) decreasing about 5' annually'. At this point on the chart the magnetic rose is tilted 11°30' west of true north to allow for accumulated variation at the time the chart was printed in 1970; thereafter magnetic north will move 5' closer to true north each year. Unless a chart is extremely old, or the annual alteration extremely high, the magnetic rose can often be used in practice as printed on a chart when navigating in a small boat, for it is impossible to steer to within a few degrees if there is any sea. In the example above, a 10-year old chart would be less than one degree adrift.

Westerly variation means that magnetic north is westward of true north, and similarly easterly variation means magnetic north is eastward of true north.

To summarise:

(1) We have looked at charts and found that they are drawn with meridians pointing to the north pole. This is *true north* and they are *true meridians* (fig 48a).

(2) We have looked at the inner rose on charts and know that it points to *magnetic north.* So too does a hand-bearing compass (fig 48b & c).

(3) We have looked at the steering compass which is subject to shipboard influences and know that it points to *compass north* (fig 48d).

(4) The difference between true north and magnetic north is called *variation.* It is due to the earth's magnetic field and is therefore the same for all ships at a particular place, but it varies from one place to another (fig 48a, b, c, d).

(5) The difference between magnetic north and compass

north is called *deviation.* It is due to influences aboard the individual boat and is therefore the same wherever she may be sailing, but is different on every course that she sails (fig 48d).

Take two boats Alpha and Beta. They are off Lowestoft, intending to sail due north. Both navigators will look up the figure for variation on their charts, apply it to the true course and find the same magnetic course. Each navigator will then look up his deviation table and find a different figure to apply to the magnetic course in order to find the compass course.

Alpha could be sailing the same course, due north, in the Azores or off New Zealand and still use the same figure for deviation, but the variation figure would be different and printed on the chart of the area. It follows that if there are several roses printed on the chart you are using, always use the nearest rose to any bearing or course you are measuring.

Beta, still off Lowestoft but this time sailing due south, will apply the same variation figure, but will have a different deviation factor due to the change in course from north to south.

Rules to Follow when Converting from True to Magnetic and from Magnetic to Compass.
Add westerly variation to true to find magnetic
Add westerly deviation to magnetic to find compass
    and similarly
Subtract easterly variation from true to find magnetic
Subtract easterly deviation from magnetic to find compass

These rules hold good, whether you are converting courses or bearings—or anything else.

To take some examples:

1) Course 225° true, variation 7°W, deviation 3°W

True course	225°
Add westerly variation	7°
Magnetic course	232°
Add westerly deviation	3°
Compass course	235°

2) Bearing 025° true, variation 12°W, deviation 2°E

True bearing	025°
Add westerly variation	12°
Magnetic bearing	037°
Subtract easterly deviation	2°
Compass bearing	035°

3) Course 005°, variation 9°E, deviation 5°W

True course	005°
Subtract easterly variation	9°
Magnetic course	356°
Add westerly deviation	5°
Compass course	001°

As you can see in the last example, when 360° or 0° is reached you continue to add clockwise or subtract anticlockwise as the case may be.

Putting this into practice (fig 49) let us suppose that you read in your book of sailing instructions that a bearing of 040° on a lighthouse, which is the limit of the arc covered by the light, leads you clear of a dangerous shoal. All bearings in the *Pilots, List of Lights, Admiralty charts, Reed's* etc. are given from seaward and are *true*. You cannot therefore pick up your hand-bearing compass, find the lighthouse bears 040° and say 'I am clear of the danger, I can steer straight for the lighthouse.' You cannot. First you must convert the true bearing of 040° to a magnetic bearing.

Looking at the inner rose you see that variation in 1969 was 12°E with only small annual alteration thereafter. Put your ruler along the line from the centre of the roses to 040° on the outer rose and you will see that this is the same as 028° on the magnetic rose, a fact which is confirmed by the calculation made according to the rule—SUBTRACT easterly variation from true to find

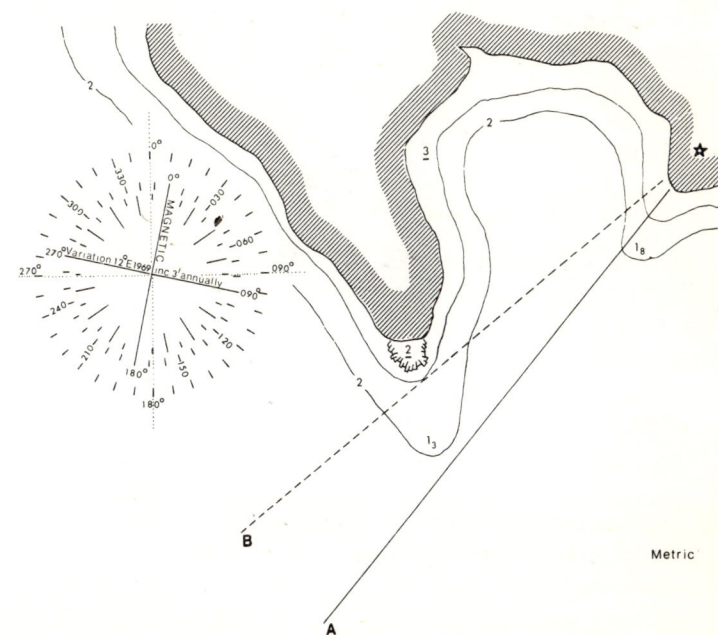

Fig.49 Bearing at *B* is 040° Magnetic as taken with the hand-bearing compass. Bearing at *A* is 040° True, 028° Magnetic.

magnetic: 040° minus 12° = 028°. This is your magnetic bearing. If you had made a mistake and relied on your hand-bearing compass bearing of 040° on the lighthouse, without correcting, you would have thought you were at *A* when in fact you were at *B*, and if you had steered for the lighthouse you would have run aground.

Suppose that from *B* you steer a more southerly course until you reach the place where the hand-bearing compass gives you the bearing 028° on the lighthouse, and that you then decide to steer a course directly along this bearing until you are clear of the head and can make for your anchorage. You need to work out your compass course. Looking up your deviation table in Appendix III you find that deviation is 4°E for this course.

Remembering the rule magnetic to compass subtract easterly deviation, you subtract 4° from the magnetic course of 028°, giving you a compass course of 024°. If it is night you will be able to check that you are on course because you will probably see the light going out from time to time as the boat moves to the waves.

So far we have worked from true to magnetic to compass. Often we have to work the opposite way, towards true.

Rules to Follow when Converting from Compass to Magnetic and from Magnetic to True.

Subtract westerly deviation from compass to find magnetic
Subtract westerly variation from magnetic to find true and similarly
Add easterly deviation to compass to find magnetic
Add easterly variation to magnetic to find true

If we point the bows of our boat exactly at an object and read our course we obtain the compass bearing of that object, say 137°. The steering compass, however, is subject to deviation and, checking in the deviation table, we see that for 135° it is 1°W. Compass to magnetic, subtract westerly deviation, so the magnetic bearing is 136°. This is also the bearing obtained with the hand-bearing compass. If we now wish to find the true bearing we check on variation, 10°W, so magnetic to true, subtract west, 136° minus 10° = true bearing 126°. Similarly:

Compass course 048°, deviation 1°W, variation 15°E

Compass course	048°
Subtract westerly deviation	1°
Magnetic course	047°
Add easterly variation	15°
True course	062°

The more you practise, the easier it is. After a winter's break you will probably find that you have forgotten the rules, so it is best to write them down in brief in any publication to which you refer frequently when plotting, and on your deviation table as well.

Look it up each time until you are absolutely sure of yourself; then you will make no disastrous mistakes.

Some people find the word

C A D E T

a useful aide-memoire. Compass to true add east.

16 : Chartwork and plotting courses

First make sure that you have a reasonable area in which to work. There are very few small boats in which you can spread out a large Admiralty chart satisfactorily, but at least clear the area of all unnecessary objects. You will often need to work at night, so think your lighting out carefully. It must be bright enough to read the small print, but the light must not glare into the helmsman's eyes.

Then consider the various alternative instruments that are available for laying off courses and bearings and, if possible, ask your friends about the disadvantages and advantages they have found in practice with the instruments they use.

(1) *Parallel Rulers.* Two rulers are attached to each other by two metal arms so they always stay parallel to each other. By opening and shutting the parallel ruler you can 'walk' a line across the chart to or from the compass roses, knowing that it is always parallel to the line from which you started (fig 50) BUT . . . and the disadvantage of parallel rulers comes in the second half of the sentence . . . only provided that the ruler has not slipped at all. It is all too easy to slip when the ruler reaches a fold in the chart or a damp patch, and once it has slipped the line is no longer parallel. One advantage of parallel rulers is that you can work on the true rose or the magnetic rose at your choice.

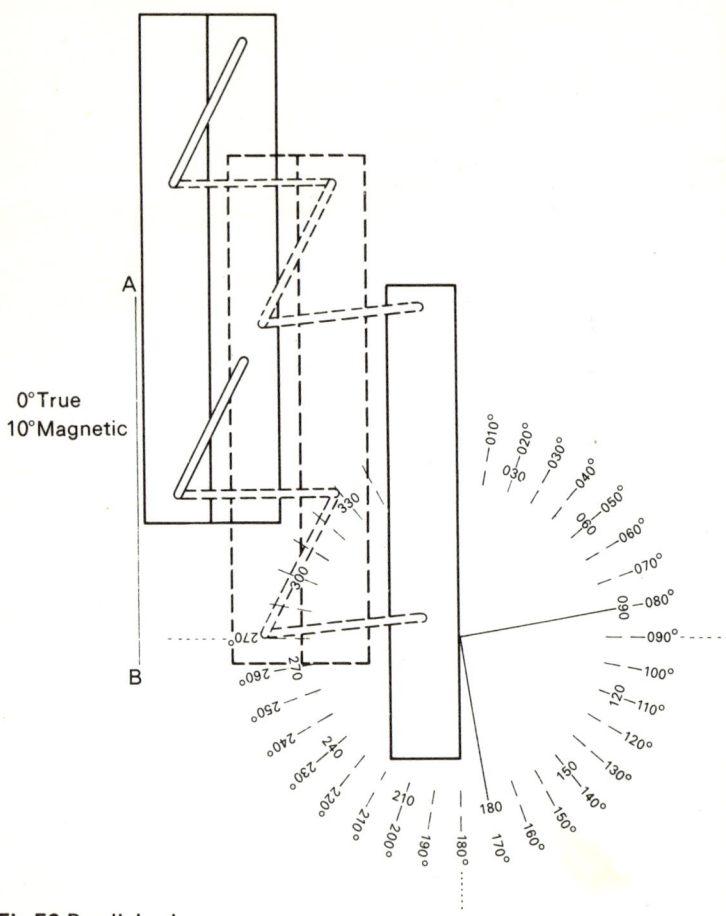

Fig.50 Parallel ruler

(2) *Protractors and Plotters.* There are several varieties on the market, each with its good points as well as its bad ones, and each with instructions on how to use it. For the most part they work on the principle of a rose with a long arm swivelling around the centre point. The rose is placed at a convenient point on the chart and turned to the correct angle to represent either the true or the magnetic rose. The arm is then swung round as required so that a bearing can either be read or drawn (fig 51).

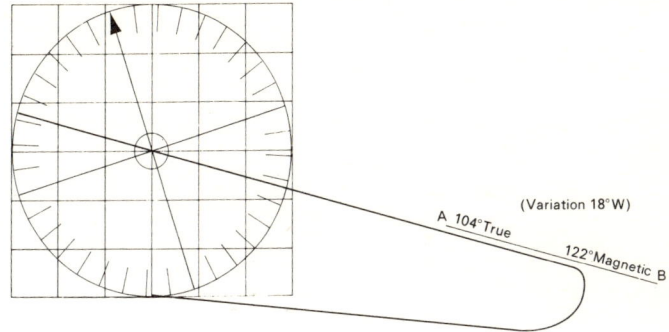

Fig.51 Hurst plotter

(3) *Plotting instruments based on the use of meridians.*
There are several methods, all of which use the meridians.
These, as we know, run true north and south, and bearings
or courses therefore have to be converted to or from true.
This becomes automatic with practice and has the added
advantage that the navigator is already thinking in terms of
the true compass when he reads a printed bearing on an
Admiralty chart, or in the *List of Lights* etc. He is
therefore less likely to make a mistake than his
counterpart who is working regularly on magnetic bearings
and courses.

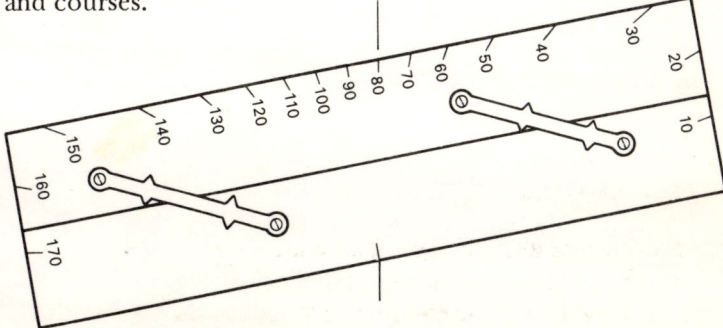

Fig.52 Captain Field's ruler

Captain Field's parallel rule is marked in degrees around
the edges and, when lined up with the south point on a
meridian, the course or bearing is read on the rule where it
cuts the same meridian (fig 52).

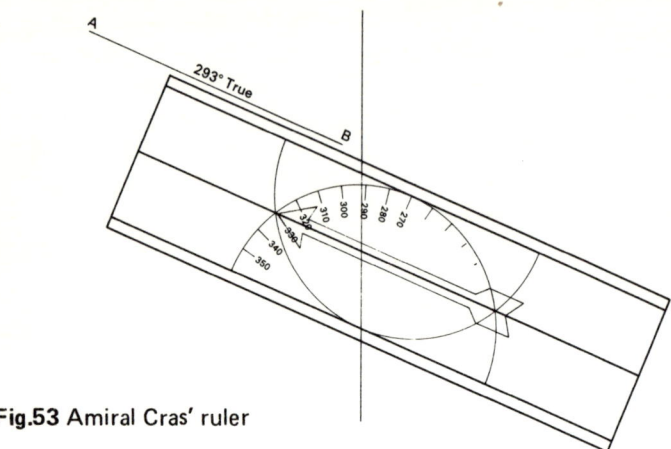

Fig.53 Amiral Cras' ruler

The French have a long broad transparent ruler, invented by Amiral Cras, with a broad arrow down the middle and two protractors on either side (fig 53). This is lined up so that the edge of the ruler is along a course or bearing, while the central point of the more southerly of the protractors is on a parallel. The bearing is read off where that parallel cuts the same protractor.

A system much used in Germany, and increasingly used in Britain, involves two rectangular equilateral set-squares, transparent, marked in degrees from a centre at the middle point of the hypotenuse (fig 54). One of the set-squares is lined up so that the centre is on a meridian,

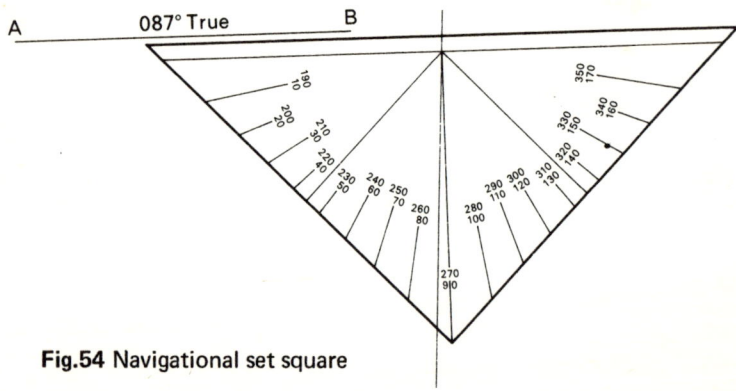

Fig.54 Navigational set square

and the bearing of a line along which the hypotenuse has been placed is read off where the same meridian cuts the rose. The unmarked edge is always used for drawing bearings, or is placed along the line of a course or a bearing. The second set-square, which need not be marked, is used as a guide along which the marked set-square can be transferred from one place to another. This is a simple and very accurate method.

Whichever instrument you choose to buy, be sure that you are quite certain whether you are basing your work on the true compass or the magnetic compass, and stick to the system you have chosen until you are really confident as a result of much practice. Later you may find another more satisfactory system.

We will use parallel rulers for the present.

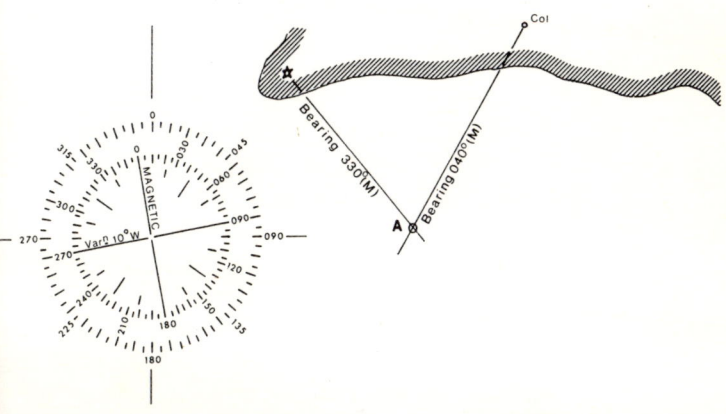

Fig.55 Laying off bearings

Laying Off Bearings Let us suppose that you have taken two bearings with your hand-bearing compass (fig 55). These are magnetic bearings. One is on a column, 040°(M), the other is on a lighthouse, 330°(M). Taking the column first, place your parallel ruler so that the edge runs from 040°, through the centre of the nearest rose to 220° (the reciprocal bearing), on the inner magnetic rose. Now 'walk' the parallel ruler over to the column and draw a line from it to seaward, from 040° towards 220°. Be careful not to let the ruler slip as you move it across the chart, especially when coming up against a fold.

Repeat the operation for the lighthouse, drawing the bearing parallel to the line on the magnetic rose 330°−150°. The position of your boat at the time you took the bearings is where the two position lines meet at A.

Because you are using a hand-bearing compass which points to magnetic north in conjunction with the magnetic compass rose on your chart there is no need to convert your bearings. Occasionally you will come across a chart which prints only a pointer to indicate magnetic north instead of a complete rose. In this case, or if you are using an instrument based on a meridian, you will need to convert your magnetic bearing to a true bearing before entering it on the chart. Magnetic to true, add east subtract west. Variation in figure 55 is 10°W in this area, so you would convert 040°(M) to 030° true, and 330°(M) to 320° true.

Note that when you pencil in your bearing you draw from the known point, the object on which you have taken your bearing, towards the waters where you are sailing. You are actually drawing the reciprocal of the bearing you have taken (that is, your bearing + or minus 180°−the other end of the same line!). This is the bearing which a man sitting on the column would take of your boat. Nine times out of ten it is obvious that you are to seaward of the object rather than in a ploughed field. The tenth time you may suddenly spot a lighthouse on an island and take a snap bearing on it. After a long hard night in misty weather, unsure of your position, and rather anxious, you can make a mistake and enter your bearing 180° wrong—with disastrous results. It has been done. So, if you are in any doubt, remember that it is the reciprocal bearing that you are drawing.

Leeway Before laying off a course we must first consider leeway. When a boat is sailing down wind all the thrust of the wind is consumed in pushing her forward through the

water and she will make no leeway. With the wind abeam a
boat sails fast forward through the water, but is also being
pushed slightly sideways: her course through the water is
not quite the same as the course she is steering, but a few
degrees to leeward. By the time a sailing boat is close
hauled her forward speed decreases and the more the
helmsman pinches the greater will be the leeway made.

Different types of boat make such different leeway that
while some navigators can safely ignore it, others could
be sailing into danger if they did so. A modern racing
yacht makes so little leeway that it need only be taken
into account when close hauled, and especially when
beating against steep short seas. On the other hand a
beamy old Dutch barge, or a motor sailer with high
topsides may make a lot of leeway when the wind is
abeam. You alone can decide how important leeway is to
you and your vessel, and the way to find out is by
watching your wake as you sail a variety of courses, in
different wind strengths. and in smooth and rough seas.
The course you are steering is a prolongation of the fore
and aft line of your boat, but the course which a boat is
making good through the water is shown by her wake (fig
56.) If the wake is streaming due aft and is itself a
prolongation of the fore and aft line, there is no leeway.
But if there is a considerable angle between two, the
boat is making considerable leeway, and you will want to
know how much. The easy answer is to take a bearing of
your wake and compare it with a bearing taken from the
bow through the mast and straight past the flagstaff.
Subtracting one from the other gives you your leeway

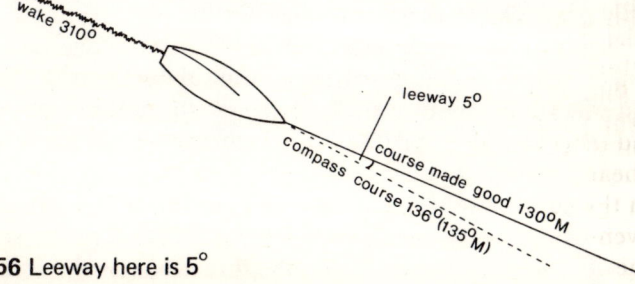

Fig.56 Leeway here is 5°

angle. More accurate is to take a bearing on your wake when the helmsman reports that he is dead on course. If you know your magnetic course, well and good; subtract the magnetic bearing of the wake, plus or minus 180°, from the magnetic course. If not, calculate your magnetic course. In figure 56 the course steered is 136° from which must be subtracted 1° westerly deviation giving a magnetic course of 135°. The wake bears 310°, subtract 180° = 130°. Leeway, therefore, is 135° less 130° = 5°.

If you are streaming a log you can use this instead of your wake when taking a bearing when it is difficult to see your wake clearly due to the state of the sea, but never use the dinghy at the end of a long painter; she will make more leeway than your sailing boat because she has no keel. Towing a dinghy will in itself increase leeway, and so does a flourishing garden of weed on the bottom of the boat, so your leeway factor will always be variable.

Laying Off a Course In figure 57 a boat intends to sail from point *A* to point *B*. The wind is W, moderate, and the time when the boat reaches *A* is 10.15. Three things must be known: the rate of the tidal stream, the set of the tidal stream, and your anticipated speed through the water.

First the tidal stream. HW Dover is 14.25 BST and from the heights given in the table it is clear that it is near neaps. The chartlet for four hours before HW Dover shows that the stream will be setting rather south of SW at a rate of 1½-2 knots from 10.25 to 11.25. There is also a letter ◇D◇ conveniently close to the area, meaning that there is a table printed on the chart giving the rate and set of the tidal stream at point *D*. This table states that at 4 hours before HW Dover the rate at neaps is 2 knots, setting 209°.

Suppose that when you reached *A* the wind dropped away entirely and you drifted on the tidal stream. At the end of an hour you would find yourself 2 miles from *A* on a bearing of 209°, true, and this is the line you now draw on the chart. True because the set of the tidal stream is given true, so use the true rose on your chart and lay off a line *AC*, 2 miles, bearing 209° from *A*. Note that the set of the tidal stream is given 209°, the direction *to* which it

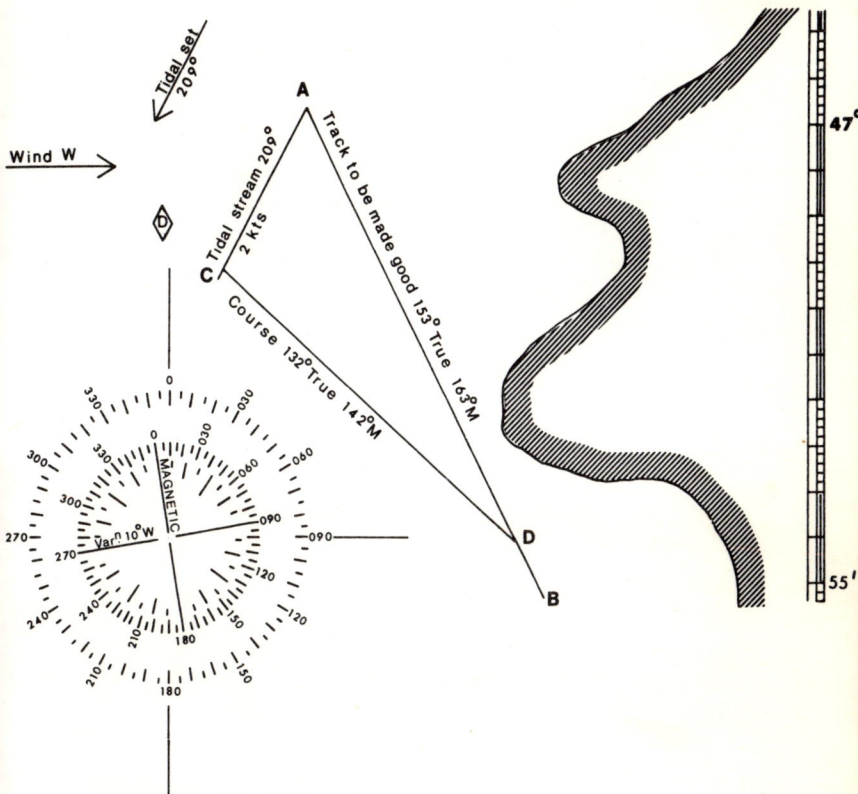

Fig.57 Plotting a course. Tidal set 209°

flows; in contrast the wind direction is given SW, the direction *from* which it blows.

During the hour, then, the effect of the tidal stream will be to set your boat 2 miles, 209°, and this must be allowed for when working out the course you will steer. You anticipate that during the same hour, with a moderate wind on your quarter, you will be sailing at 4½ knots, and will therefore travel 4½ miles through the water. Using the side margin parallel to *AB* measure 4½ miles and from point *C* mark your line *AB* at point *D*, 4½ miles from *C*. Join *CD* which is the course you must steer, allowing for the tidal stream, if you want to make good the course *ADB*.

If you find the bearing of *CD* by using the true rose you will get a figure of 132° to which you must add 10° westerly variation to find the magnetic course (true to magnetic add west): if you use the inner magnetic rose you obtain the magnetic course of 142° immediately. This must now be converted to a compass course by allowing for deviation, taken from the sample table in Appendix 3.

Magnetic course	142°
Add westerly deviation	1°
Compass course	143°

With the wind abaft the beam there is no leeway to take into account, so the compass course is also the course to steer, 143°.

Figure 58 shows how the boat will move along the line *AB* during the course of the hour. You will often need to know when you will reach a particular point, perhaps *E*

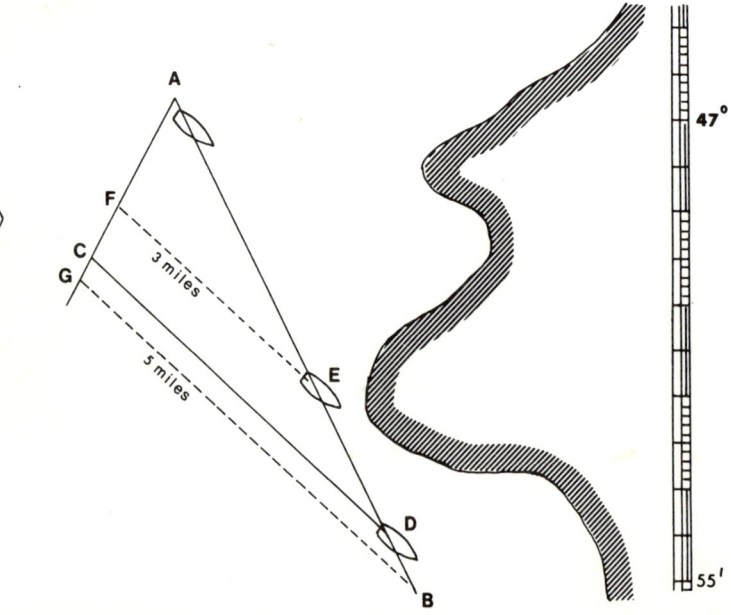

Fig.58 How the boat moves along her course *AB*

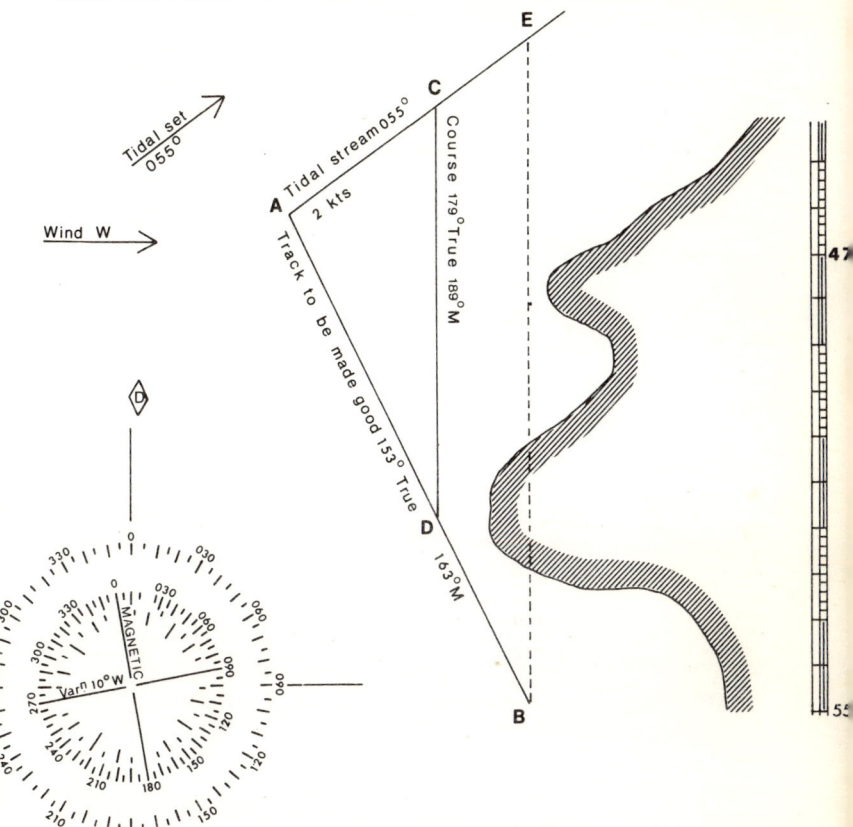

Fig.59 Plotting a course, tidal set 055°

when the boat is close to the headland, perhaps point *B* itself. From point *E* draw a line parallel to your course which meets the line *AC* representing the tidal stream at *F*. *FE* is 3 miles. Your boat is sailing at 4½ knots so will take 40 minutes to cover 3 miles and your expected time of arrival at *E* is 10.55. Similarly *GB* is 5 miles so, at 4½ knots, the boat should reach *B* at 11.22.

Figure 59 is based on the same stretch of coast, the same wind, W moderate, the same rate of tidal stream, 2 knots, but the set is different, 055°. The course to be steered alters drastically. *AC* represents the tidal set from 10.15 to 11.15 and *CD* the course if the boat is sailing at 4½ knots, 179° true, 189° magnetic. To this must be added 4° westerly deviation (see Appendix 3) giving a compass course of 193°. With the wind abeam the boat may well make 2° of leeway, and the boat will therefore have to sail 2° closer to the wind, giving a course to steer of 195°. And what of your time of arrival at *B?* The distance from *E* to *B* is 7¼ miles, so at 4½ knots you would arrive there about 11.55. The line *EB* crosses the more southerly head, but this does not matter because the actual track that your boat will be sailing through the water is, of course, *AB*.

Plotting A Course for a Longer Period Instead of a mere hour's sail, a boat may be setting off on a much longer trip, and the navigator has to set a course for the first three hours or so. Unless there are dangers to be avoided a course can often be set for the whole three hours by working out the cumulative effect of the tidal stream. In figure 60 the track to be made good, *AB,* is 270° magnetic, and there is a nice NW breeze. Looking up the tidal stream you find that the set is constant throughout the three hours, 030°, but that the rate varies: 1st hour 2 knots, 2nd hour 3 knots, 3rd hour 3 knots. Adding these together gives a total set of 8 miles 030° during the 3 hours. Your anticipated average speed is 6 knots, so you expect to cover 18 miles in the 3 hours. To make good track *AB* you will sail course *CD,* 250° magnetic. Adding 3° westerly deviation gives you a compass course of 253°, but with the wind almost abeam leeway might be 2° bringing the course to steer to 255°.

Figure 61 shows how to allow for a tidal stream which sets differently in each of the three hours. From *A*, the boat's position when plotting the course, draw a line *AC* to represent the set of the tidal stream in the first hour, 3 miles 209°. From *C* draw *CD* to show the second hour's set, 4 miles 170°, and from *D* draw *DE*, 2 miles 155°, the third hour's set. You expect to sail at 5 knots during the

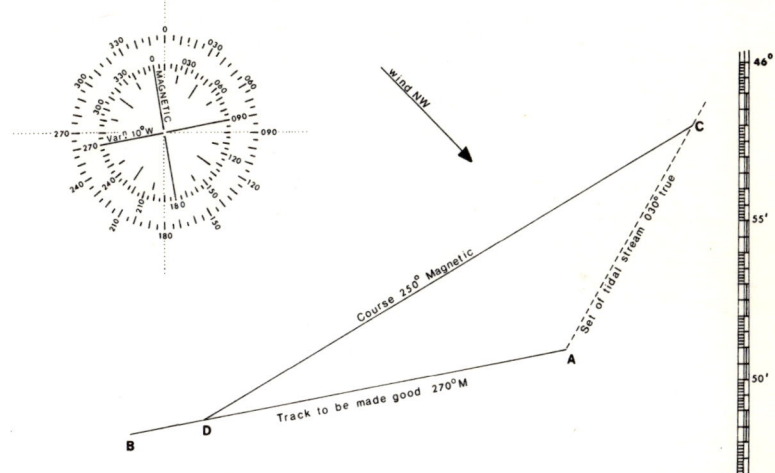

Fig.60 Plotting a course, tidal set 030° for three hours

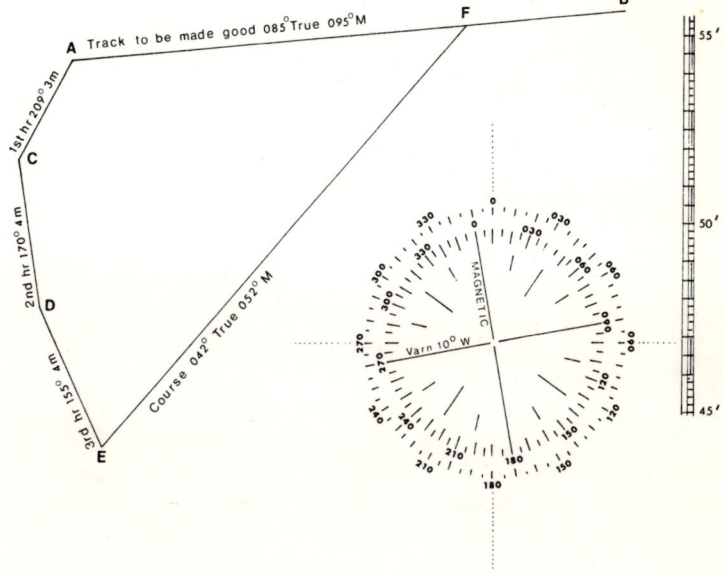

Fig.61 Plotting a course, tidal set varies for three hours

three hours so should cover 15 miles. From point *E* measure 15 miles with your dividers and mark the line *AB* at *F*. To make good *AB* you must sail course *EF*, 042° true, 052° magnetic.

It may be that you are sailing along the coast and that you start with a foul tidal stream which turns in the third hour of a five hour trip. There is a set of 100°, 1½ knots in the first hour and ½ knot in the second. In the third hour set and rate are uncertain. In the fourth and fifth hours set is reversed, 280°, ½ knot in the fourth hour increasing to 1 knot in the fifth. As your course and the tidal stream set coincide, you can simplify your plotting by reckoning that you will suffer an adverse set of 2 miles in the first two hours and will later reap the benefit of 1½ miles favourable set. So over the five hours you can expect a total reduction of ½ mile to your distance sailed through the water (fig 62). It may happen that you later have to break your plotting down into hours as in the lower line, but the top method is so much easier!

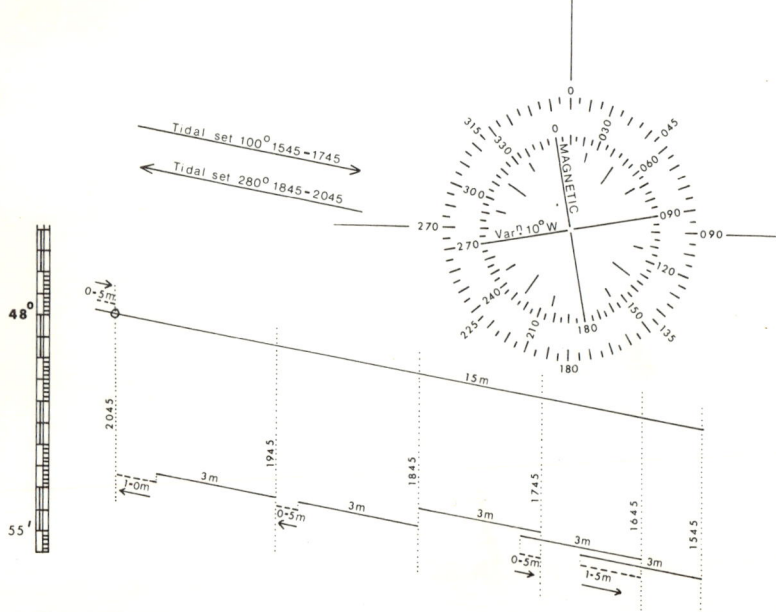

Fig.62 Plotting a course, tidal set reverses

That was a stream setting dead against you or with you. If the stream is setting across your course you can sometimes take a short cut with your plotting. Suppose you are intending to cross the Channel to Cherbourg—a distance of some 60 miles—and you expect to sail at about 5 knots with the wind moderate, abeam. This is very convenient, and is also often the case, for the duration of a full ebb stream and flood stream cycle is 12 hours—the length of time you take to cross the Channel at 5 knots.

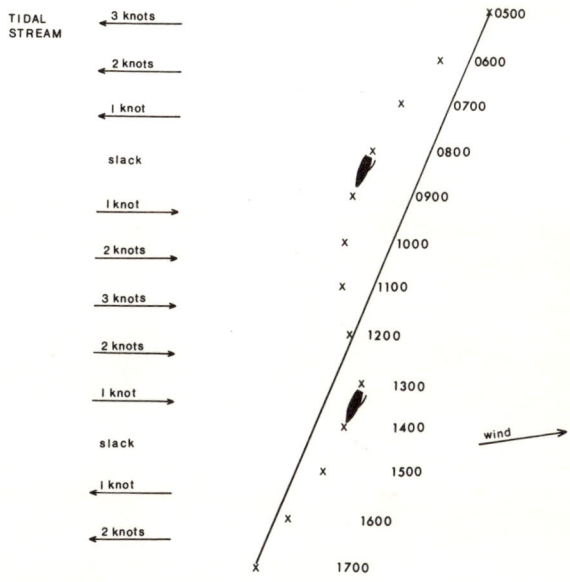

Fig.63 Plotting a course with twelve hours of cross streams

For six of those hours the west-going stream will be setting your boat westward, and for another six hours the east-going stream will be setting her eastward, so they cancel each other out. You can set course direct for your destination and keep your fingers crossed that the wind holds and that you maintain your 5 knot average speed. During the twelve hours the actual position will only momentarily be on the direct course from your departure point to your arrival point, at 12.00 hrs in figure 63. At

0800 you will be 6 miles to westward and at 1500 you will be 3 miles to the east.

Should the wind and your speed through the water increase you will reach your destination earlier, say about 15.50 hrs. so when you realise that this is likely to be the case you will need to sail rather closer to the wind to avoid being set too far to the east. Equally, if the wind eases and you realise you are going to take somewhat longer than 12 hours, you know that the tidal stream will be setting you to the west during the remaining hours of your trip, so you need to bear away to compensate.

In plotting courses we are working with a series of variables. First the tidal streams: the figures we find in chartlets or on the chart are based on statistics gathered over the years and are average figures. As with all such figures they are subject to modification due to meteorological conditions. Then there is the wind: we may state SW moderate, but it is rare for the wind to remain completely constant in direction or strength for a full hour—or even for ten minutes. At times it will strengthen, at times it will ease or blow from a slightly different direction, and all this will affect the speed of the boat through the water. Then there is the sea: you may find on approaching a headland that you meet very rough water which slows the boat down very considerably—or a patch of surprisingly calm water in the lee of some land. Leeway may alter very considerably according to the seas met.

And then there is the helmsman himself: you may give him a course to steer, but the course he actually does steer is often very different. Steer SE is a clear concise instruction, but if there is anything of a sea a good helmsman is bound to ease the boat over the worst crests if he wants to sail her at her best, and this may well mean that the course is in fact nearer ESE or SSE. Collaboration is the answer. The navigator gives the optimum course but, unless it is a case of racing or to avoid some danger, he does not expect absolute accuracy in carrying out his instructions. He must then make his instructions especially clear and be sure that the helmsman has understood the reason for the course. On a long cross channel course he can tell the helmsman to steer as near south by west as is comfortable, but on approaching the Alderney Race he will give a more exact course and expect the helmsman to steer it accurately. When the helmsman knows the reason for accuracy his concentration improves no end!

A helmsman must also be encouraged to report honestly the course that he has actually steered, rather than the course he would like to claim to have steered. There are optimistic helmsmen who think they have steered 5° closer to the wind on a beat than actually was the case. The wise navigator will check the helmsman's performance whenever he has an opportunity and compare it with the course reported later.

17 : Fixing the boat's position

It has just been mentioned that some of the figures on which calculations are based when plotting courses are averages or approximations; sometimes they are guesswork. There is also the variability of the natural conditions to take into account, and lastly there is human error. It follows that the navigator needs every clue that he can get to establish the position of his boat accurately, and he will then not only know where he is but will also be able to check how well he has plotted his course.

Known Positions. When a boat passes close by a buoy, a light vessel, or a beacon the navigator knows exactly where he is, and by noting the time and the log reading he has a definite position from which to plot his onward course.

Where two transits meet, the navigator can fix the boat's position with certainty because there is no room for error provided the objects have been properly identified. It may be well worth while deliberately sailing along one transit until a second is reached in order to establish your position with accuracy as in figure 36, for one can then take the opportunity to check the deviation of the steering compass or the accuracy of bearings taken with the hand-bearing compass.

Position Lines The use of position lines has been mentioned already in chapter 9. To summarise and elaborate:

(1) *Transits.* When two or more objects are in line with each other, they give an excellent position line. For example, the two marks or lights of a leading line, the two marks of a measured mile, two conspicuous buildings ashore, two natural features such as a headland and a rock, a natural feature and a building, or a long sewer outfall or pier at the moment when it points directly to the boat. The essential point is that the objects must be marked on the chart.

(2) *Bearings.* A bearing on any object marked on the chart gives a position line, and preferably should be taken on a fixed object rather than a floating one if there is a choice. It is rare for buoys or light-vessels to be found out of position, but it can happen due to collision or exceptional weather conditions.

The essential point is to identify the object on which you are taking a bearing. If, for example, there is any doubt in your mind as to which white house is the one marked on the chart, take bearings of both and note them, together with time and log reading. Subsequent observation may make it obvious which white house is the one on the chart.

(3) *Radio bearings.* If you carry the right equipment you can obtain a position line by tuning in to a transmitting beacon.

(4) *Soundings.* The depth of water in which you are sailing can be used to give you a position line.

(5) *Angles.* If you have a sextant and know how to use it you can measure angles which will give you a curved position line. The most simple use is measuring the angle of a lighthouse above the foreshore to give you the distance off the light.

(6) *Range of a light.* The moment when you raise the light on a lighthouse gives you a circular position line. The range of such lights is given in the *List of Lights,* in *Reed's* and on charts, and is stated in terms of an observer 5 metres above sea level. In a small boat where the observer is only a few feet above sea level the range is reduced by approximately 1½ miles. Thus South Foreland, with a range of 25 miles, would be raised by a small boat anywhere on the circumference of a circle with a radius of 23½ miles, centred on South Foreland. Add a bearing on the light and the boat's position is fixed (fig 64).

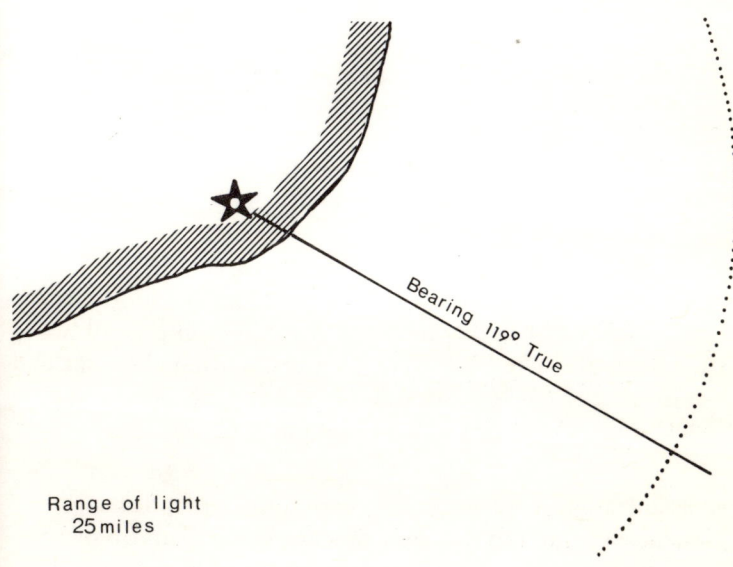

Bearing 119° True

Range of light
25 miles

Fig.64 Fix, using the range of a light and a bearing

(7) *Sectors of a light*. The change from one colour to another occurs on a known bearing, true, so when you see a light change colour due to sailing from one sector into another you have a good position line.

Any two position lines can be used for fixing the position of a boat.

Cross Bearings Two bearings which cross each other will give you a good idea as to your whereabouts, but if you are to get a good fix you will need to select with care the objects on which you take your bearings. Sometimes, of course, there is no choice and any bearing is better than none.

First: a more accurate fix is obtained when two bearings are roughly at right angles to each other. In figure 65a the bearings on the ruins and the windmill intersect nearly at right angles and, if taken with absolute accuracy, the position of the boat is where they cross. In a small boat it is not easy to be absolutely accurate, so if you allow for a possible 5° of error in both bearings your possible position could be anywhere within the darker hatched lines.

Compare this area with figure 65b where the bearings were taken on the ruins and a radio mast and meet at a much greater angle. The area in which the boat may possibly be is very much greater.

In figure 65c three bearings have been taken, one on each object. Three such bearings rarely meet exactly due to the problems of taking bearings accurately in a small boat, but form a 'cocked hat'. The chances are that the boat will be inside the cocked hat and, obviously, the smaller the cocked hat the better you will be pleased.

Second: a more accurate fix is obtained when bearings are taken on relatively close objects rather than on distant ones because the area of error increases with distance. In figures 66a and 66b the angle between the tower and the monument is the same as that between the monument and the ramark. The ramark is twice as far from the boat as the

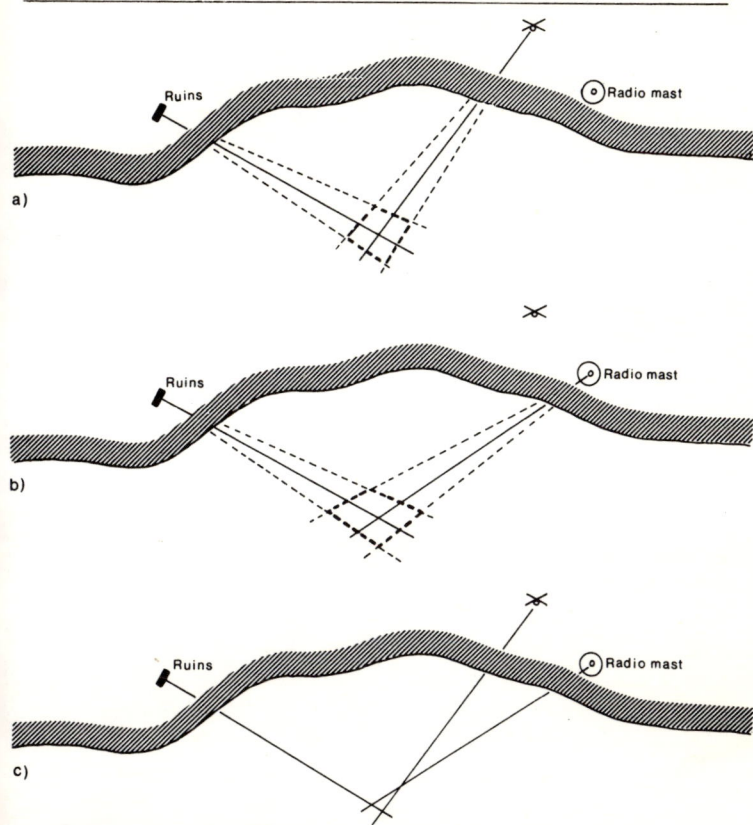

Fig.65 Cross bearings. The area in which a boat may be, allowing for a 5° error in taking the bearing, is smaller if the two bearings are nearly at right angles.

tower, and the possible area, allowing for 5° error, is in consequence about twice the size (fig 66b).

In theory bearings should be taken simultaneously because the boat is moving while you are taking them. If you are sailing in a 5 knot favourable tidal stream and making 5 knots through the water yourself you will cover half a mile in three minutes. The time at which the bearings are taken should be noted when you take the one that changes most rapidly, whether it is the one that is most nearly abeam, or the one that alters most rapidly as you are whisked past by a strong stream or current. The

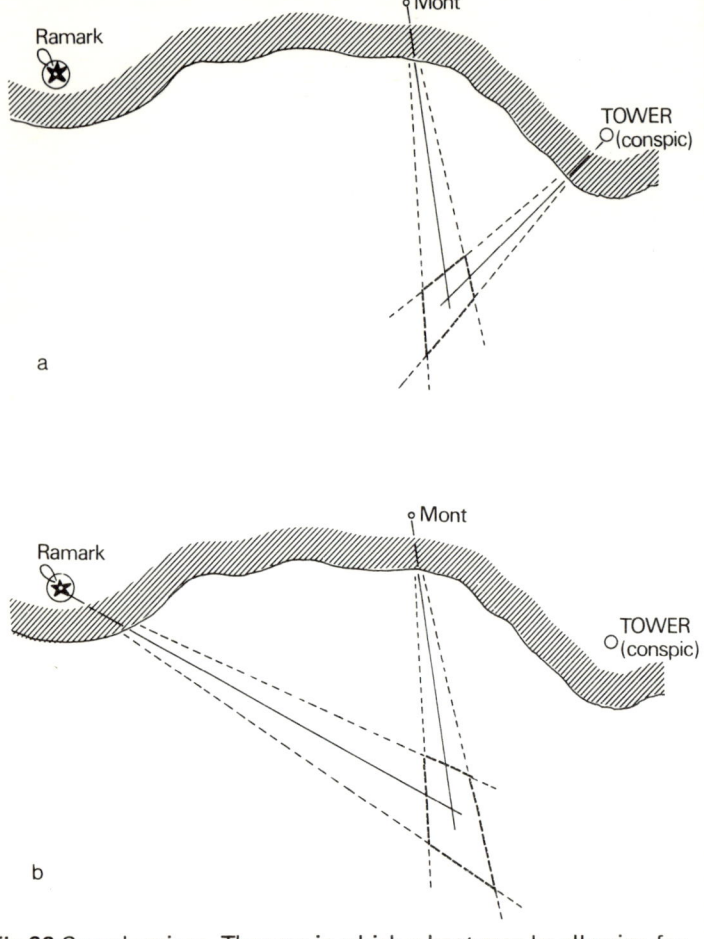

Fig.66 Cross bearings. The area in which a boat may be allowing for a 5° error in taking the bearings, is smaller if bearings are not too far distant.

bearing that changes least can be taken last and will not have changed appreciably while you were at work. Thus in figure 65c if you are sailing away from the ruins, first note the time, then take the bearing on the windmill, follow with the radio mast and finish with the ruins.

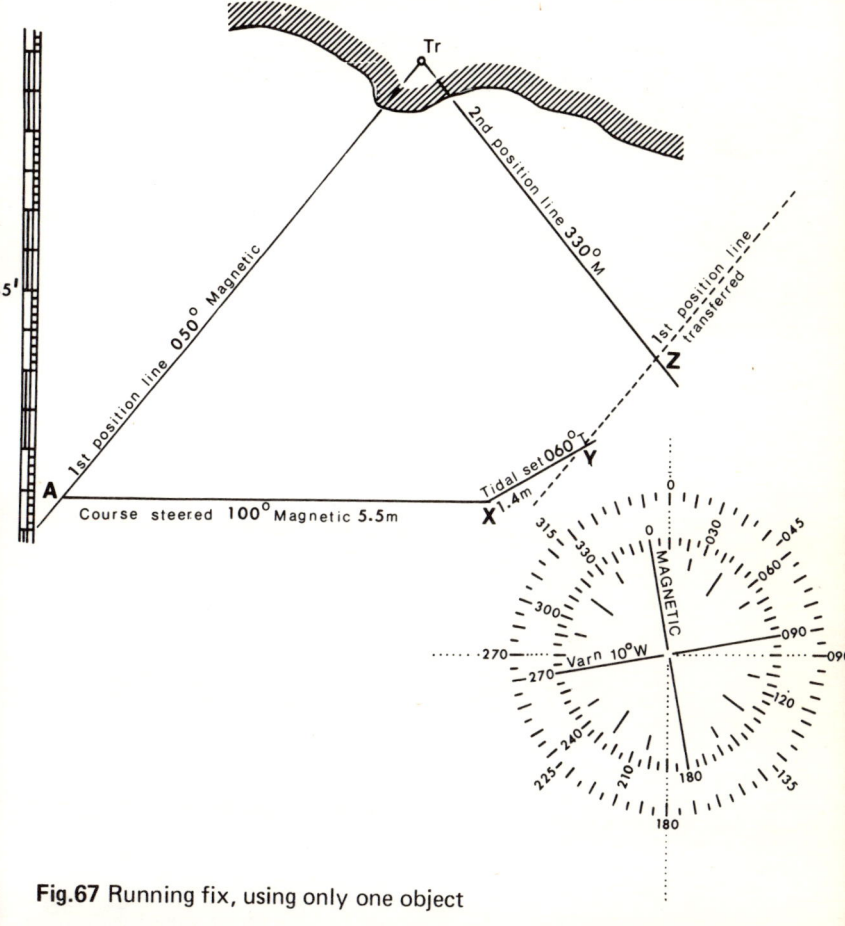

Fig.67 Running fix, using only one object

Running Fix The coast is not always so co-operative. You may well find that instead of three objects on which to take bearings you have only one, in this case a tower (fig 67). This time two bearings will be taken of the same object, and the distance sailed between taking bearings has to be calculated. At 1215 a bearing is taken on the tower, 050° magnetic, the log reading is noted, 24.4, and the boat is then carefully sailed on a compass course of 98°. An hour later a second bearing on the tower reads 330°, log 29.9 miles.

Enter the first bearing of 050°; this is your first position line. From any point *A* on this first position line draw the course sailed through the water. No leeway, compass course 98°, deviation 2°E gives a magnetic course of 100° The boat has sailed 5.5 miles through the water since taking the first bearing, so *AX* is 5.5 miles long. The tidal stream must now be allowed for 060°, 1.4 knots. *XY* is drawn 060° true, 1.4 miles to represent the set during the hour. Now draw a line through *Y,* parallel to the first position line. Enter the second bearing on the tower, 330° on the chart. This is your second position line. The point *Z*, where the second position line cuts the transferred first position line, is the position of the boat at 13.15.
The same system can be adopted in the case of two

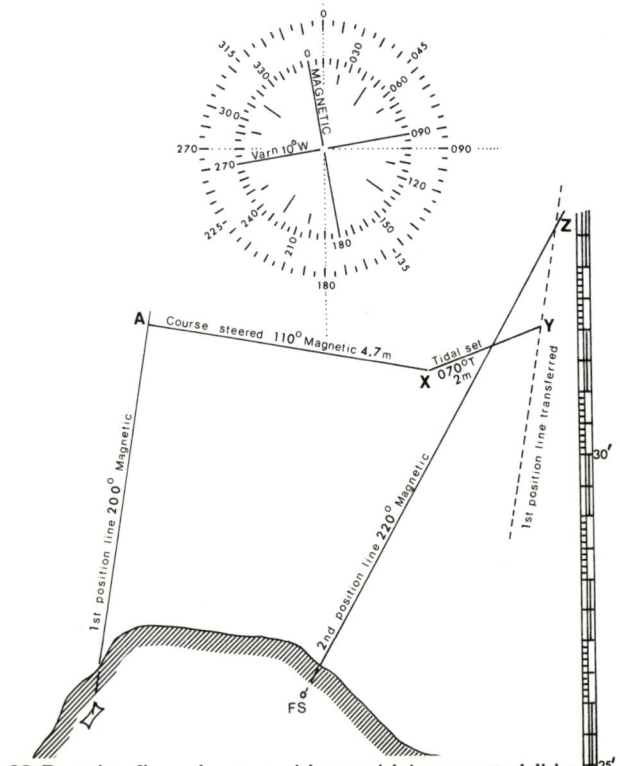

Fig.68 Running fix, using two objects which are not visible simultaneously

different objects which are not visible simultaneously. In figure 68 a boat is approaching a headland, and a fort bears 200° magnetic at 13.30, at which time the log reads 32.2 miles. Passing the head your carefully sailed compass course of 109° brings you in sight of a flagstaff at 14.15 which bears 220°, at which moment the log reads 36.9 miles. Leeway again is negligible.

The first position line is entered on the chart, 200°, the bearing on the fort, and the course is drawn from A, somewhere along that position line. 109° compass course, plus 1° easterly deviation, gives a magnetic course of 110°. AX is 4.7 miles, the distance logged. Now for the tidal stream which has been setting 070° true at 2.6 knots. The line XY is drawn 070° 2 miles, the distance the boat has been set in three-quarters of an hour. Transfer the first position line as before, parallel and passing through Y. Now enter the second bearing, 220° on the flagstaff. The position of the boat at 14.15 is Z, where the second bearing cuts the transferred position line.

In both these cases the positions are less reliable than those obtained by cross bearings because the set and rate of the tidal stream is always an uncertain factor and can only be estimated. The boat's course through the water should be reasonably accurate if the helmsman is asked to steer attentively.

Fix by Bearing and Transit This is a particularly reliable fix, because one of the two position lines must be 100 per cent accurate.

Doubling the Angle on the Bow This again is a method of fixing the position of a boat by means of two bearings taken on a single object, but this time the bearings are related to her course.

Digging out a perhaps rusty memory of geometry from the subconscious the isosceles triangle appears: a triangle with two equal sides and two equal angles. In figure 69 angle CAB = angle ACB, and AB = CB. The triangle ABC is an isosceles triangle. Angle CBD = angle BAC + angle BCA, so

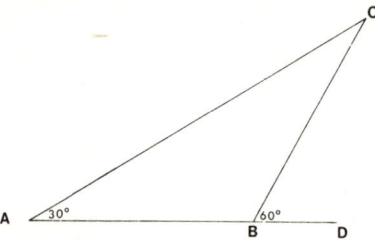

Fig.69 Isosceles triangle

angle *CBD* is double angle *CAB*. If this is applied as in figure 70 the line *AB* is the boat's course and *C* is a monument slightly inland. There are some rocks off the headland and you need to know your distance off—that is, the distance from your boat to the headland. This can be established before you reach the danger by doubling the angle on the bow, provided the tidal stream is virtually with you or against you as it is in figure 70 where the rate is one knot.

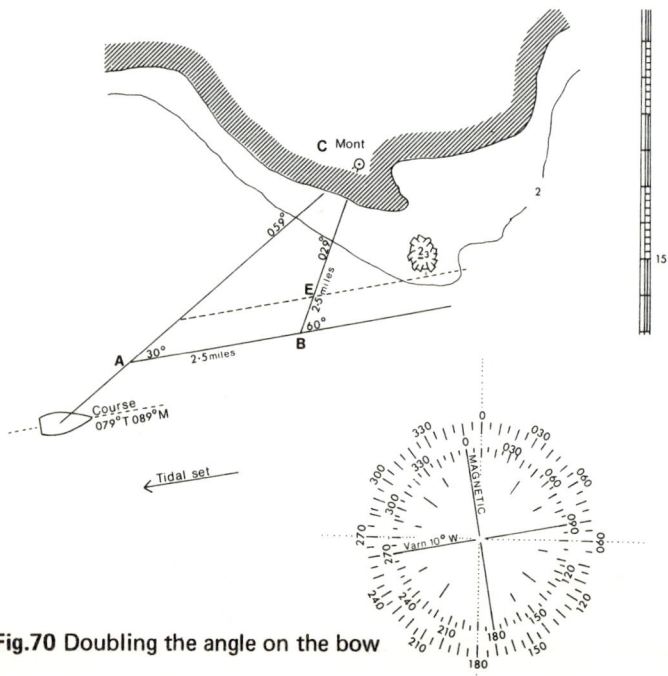

Fig.70 Doubling the angle on the bow

The boat is sailing a magnetic course of 089°, and at 12.15, with the log reading 24.5, the monument bears 059° magnetic. It is 30° on your port bow (magnetic course 089° minus 059°). The boat sails steadily on, keeping carefully on course, until the bearing on the monument is 029° magnetic at which moment it is 60° on her port bow, double the first angle. The time is 12.45 and the log reads 27.5 By calculating the distance the boat has sailed over the ground you can find the distance off, which will be the same distance. In the half hour the boat has logged 3 miles, but there has been an adverse tidal stream running at 1 knot, so the distance made good is 2.5 miles, and this is also the distance of the boat from the monument, so she is at point B. Continuing on her present course she will clear the rocks by about half a mile. But suppose that you have underestimated the rate of the tidal stream which turned earlier than expected or suppose that the log is over-reading. With a tidal rate of 2 knots the boat would be set back one mile and would only have made good 2 miles in the half hour.

Consequently her distance off would also be 2 miles putting her at point E. If she continued on her course she would be dangerously near the rock. It is as well to take a cautious view when estimating the effect of the tidal stream and distance made good and to allow a safety margin. In figure 70 the boat would do well to head further out to sea for a while.

Four-point Bearing This is just the same as doubling the angle on the bow, but the first bearing is taken when the object is 45° to the boat's course. The second bearing at 90° to your course is when the object is abeam. The disadvantage is obviously that distance off is not established until the headland and the dangers off it are abeam. Just as when fixing your position by doubling the angle on the bow, a four-point bearing should only be used when the tidal stream is setting with you or against you, and when sailing along the coast it usually is. A great advantage of these methods of position fixing is that you can use any object on land to establish distance off. A prominent tree close by the shore, a break in the cliffs or a conspicuous rock will do provided that you take both bearings on the same object. There is no need for it to be marked on the chart.

Soundings In certain areas soundings can be used to provide a position line. If there is a large expanse of water, all much the same depth, a sounding cannot help to fix your position, and equally, if there are a large number of places dotted around the chart, all of similar depth, one sounding cannot be useful. But it may be that you are sailing along a coast that shelves gradually and regularly. You can then combine a sounding with a bearing to fix your position.

Suppose that, as in figure 71, you take a bearing on a house and at the same time take a sounding which gives you a depth of 7.2 metres. This will have to be reduced to chart datum, and the accurate way of doing this is by using the Admiralty *Tide Tables*. This is not a ploy for

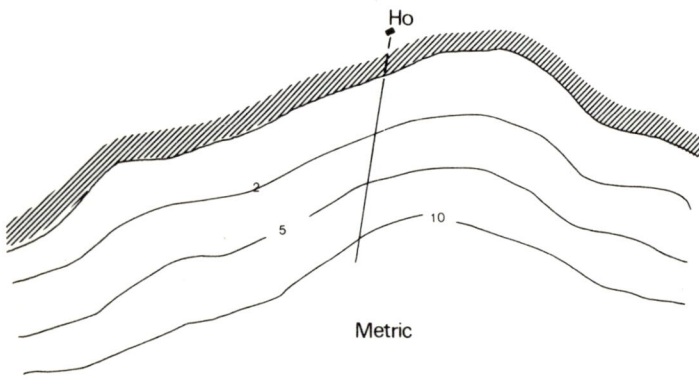

Fig.71 Fix by sounding and bearing

navigators still wearing L-plates, and those who are getting more familiar with navigation may well prefer to use *Reed's Rise and Fall Tables* and the detailed instructions with it. For our part we will use the rough and ready twelfths rule, 1:2:3:3:2:1 which is better than nothing.

First the range must be established. If both HW and LW are printed in your tide table you can find the day's range easily by subtracting the LW height from the preceding or following HW height. HW 3.5 metres, LW 0.5 metres, range 3 metres. For some ports only the daily HW is given and in this case the LW height has to be calculated. Mean tide level is given for all ports—the half-way mark of all tides, springs or neaps (see fig 4). To find LW take the Mean Tide Level, multiply by two subtract the HW height for the day. Thus

Mean Tide Level	2 metres
Multiply by 2	4 metres
Subtract HW height	3.5 metres
LW height	0.5 metres

The time when you took your sounding was 2 hours before HW so you know that the depth of water will normally be greater by 9/12ths of the range than chart datum plus LW height (1st hour after LW 1/12th, 2nd hour 2/12ths, 3rd and 4th hours 3/12ths each). Nine twelfths of 3 metres is 2.25 metres and your sounding was 7.2 metres, so chart datum would be 7.2 less 2.25 less 0.5 = 4.50 metres, and your approximate position would be slightly inshore of the point where your bearing crosses the 5 metre contour.

Running a Line of Soundings A position can sometimes be found when the contours of the bottom are suitable by noting a succession of soundings while steering a constant course, and with an echo-sounder aboard this is no longer a cold, wet undertaking. A suitable sea-bed this time is one which changes considerably and is irregular in depth. This method of position fixing is particularly useful in poor visibility when bearings cannot be taken.

A steady course is steered, and soundings taken every half mile or so over the ground. In figure 72 the boat is sailing at 6 knots with a negligible tidal stream, so a sounding is taken every 5 minutes. The figures are then

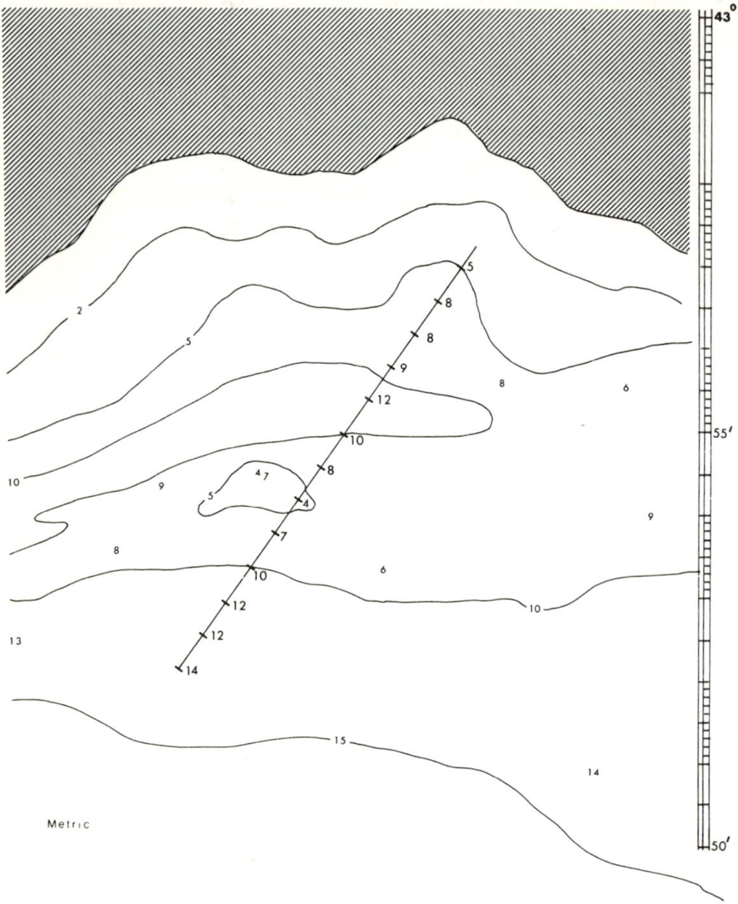

Fig.72 Running a line of soundings

reduced to chart datum and read 14, 12, 12, 10, 7, 4, 8, 10, 12, 9, 8, 8 and 5. On a piece of tracing paper or along the edge of a straight-sided piece of paper enter the soundings to the same scale as the chart. Holding the paper at the same angle as your course made good you can move it around the chart until you find an area where the soundings match up with your figures—but beware—there may be more than one area which matches.

D. F. Bearings These are invaluable in misty conditions and when out of sight of land, but they are no more free from error than any other bearings. Some of the errors can be caused by intervening land, night effect, too close or too distant a beacon and, as always, possible crew error. *Reed's* gives good advice, and there are several excellent books on the subject as well as the instructions which accompany the D.F. sets. The same applies to Decca, Consol and Loran Radio Ship Position Finding Systems.

18 : Keeping a log, dead reckoning and planning passages

Conditions change constantly at sea: the wind strengthens, changes direction and can cause you to alter course; the tidal stream can be unexpectedly vigorous; the sea may be steep and confused; you may have to change sail. All and any of these things should be entered in the log, together with everything that will help you fix your position.

When you are sailing in sight of land it is much easier to plot the ship's track because you can see the shore and how you are moving in relation to it. You will sight objects on which you can take bearings. You know, at least roughly, where you are. At sea, with no land in view, you will need to rely on dead reckoning—unless you are a dab hand with a sextant in which case you will be too skilled to be reading this book! In a way dead reckoning, which is really deduced reckoning, is like course plotting in reverse. When plotting a course you decide where you want to go, allow for the tidal stream, estimate your speed, find the magnetic course, convert to a compass course, allow for leeway and, hey presto—you have the course to steer.

To plot your track made good you start with the course you have steered, allow for leeway, convert to magnetic and note the distance logged. This gives you your D.R. position. Then allow for the tidal stream and you can plot your estimated position and draw in the line which shows the track of the boat over the ground, the track made good.

To establish accurately the course steered you must note all that occurs. Suggested headings for your log book are:

(1) *Time*. This is all-important. It is satisfying to be able to fix your position exactly by sailing close to a beacon, but it will be of no use to you later in your sail unless you have also noted the time at which you passed it.

(2) *Log*. You will also need to know how far you sailed from your beacon. A note should be made of the log reading whenever you fix your position, change course, note a major change in wind direction or strength and especially one which affects your speed, take a bearing etc. and the log reading should be noted at least hourly.

(3) *The Course Made Good*. The course you have actually sailed over the ground. You establish it either by dead reckoning as described later or by drawing a line from a last known position to a new fix.

(4) *Distance Made Good*. The distance you have actually sailed over the ground to your new position.

(5) *The Wind*. All changes in wind direction and strength should be noted, with time and log reading, and additionally note the wind direction and force when you read the log hourly.

(6) *The Barometer*. Regular readings are a great help in forecasting weather.

(7) *The Course to Steer*. Make a note of the course you have given the helmsman to steer. You may need to refer to it. Also, when you brood at home over the success or failure of your navigation after your trip you will find it useful to compare the course you set with the course made good. It is best to note down your figures for variation,

deviation, leeway and tidal stream rate and set. In your armchair at home you will quickly spot any errors you have made under less favourable conditions at sea.

(8)   *Notes.* Take notes on everything that may affect your course and speed. All bearings on objects should be included, whether they have given you a fix or not. One position line is always better than none—provided you made a note of the time you took the bearing, the log reading and your subsequent course. You may later be able to transfer it for a running fix. Other items worth noting are shipping lanes, raising a distant light, losing sight of land as you sail seaward, altering course to avoid another vessel etc.

Dead Reckoning D.R. will be easy having worked out how to take a running fix, for the principle is the same. You have set a course to steer and an hour later decide to work out your estimated position. At the start of that hour you knew exactly where you were so you can at this stage start from a definite position. Irrespective of the course that you told the helmsman to steer ask him what course he reckons he has been steering during the past hour. If you are beating and he has been trying to get as far to windward as possible allow for the fact that he may be over-optimistic unless he is pretty experienced. Indeed, if he has been pointing very high the leeway that he has made will almost certainly be greater than you allowed for. Whenever you are on deck you will yourself make a mental note of the course being steered, and also the leeway, so you can judge the accuracy of his estimate yourself. Of course a lot depends on how seriously your helmsman is taking his job. Having been caught 180° off course when on watch with my then future husband . . . but that was one of those errors which a navigator can hardly be expected to anticipate!

From your last known position draw a line to represent the course steered, having allowed for leeway and optimism and having converted from compass to magnetic. Using dividers, measure along this line the distance logged.

E

Now the tidal stream. From that point draw a line to represent the set and rate. This gives you your estimated position. Note the time and the log reading in your log and also on the chart; you can then plot on from there. You will need to work out your estimated position every time you alter course.

Crossing a bay using dead reckoning. Setting out to cross a broad bay, the distant and low-lying shores of which will give no opportunity of taking bearings to fix the boat's position, the navigator has to rely on dead reckoning as in figure 73.

He reaches buoy *A* at 10.15 and calculates that the direct track to buoy *B*, some 28 miles distant, is 195° magnetic. The set of the tidal stream for the first two hours is virtually dead against him, 010°, at a rate of 1.5 knots in the first hour and 0.5 knots in the second, with the stream easing to nil at slack water. During the following six hours the tidal stream will be fair: 190°, 12.15 0.5 kts: 13.15 1.5 kts: 200°, 14.15 1.5 kts: 15.15 1.7 kts: 180°, 16.15 1 knot: 17.15 0.8 kts. The wind is abeam, moderate W. Variation in the area is 10°W.

Working out the course to steer he reckons that with the tidal stream cancelling itself out in the first hours, and virtually along his track, he need only adjust the magnetic course for deviation and for leeway:

Magnetic course	195°
Deviation 4° W	4°
	199°
Leeway 3° (to windward)	3°
Course to steer	202°

At *J*, close by buoy *A* he reads the log, 15, enters this, the time 10.15, plus the weather and wind details in the log book. During the next four hours he is off watch asleep, but the helmsman records the hourly readings of the log: 19.7, 24.2, 28.5 and 31.0. There is a note that in the last hour the wind has backed to SW and eased slightly.

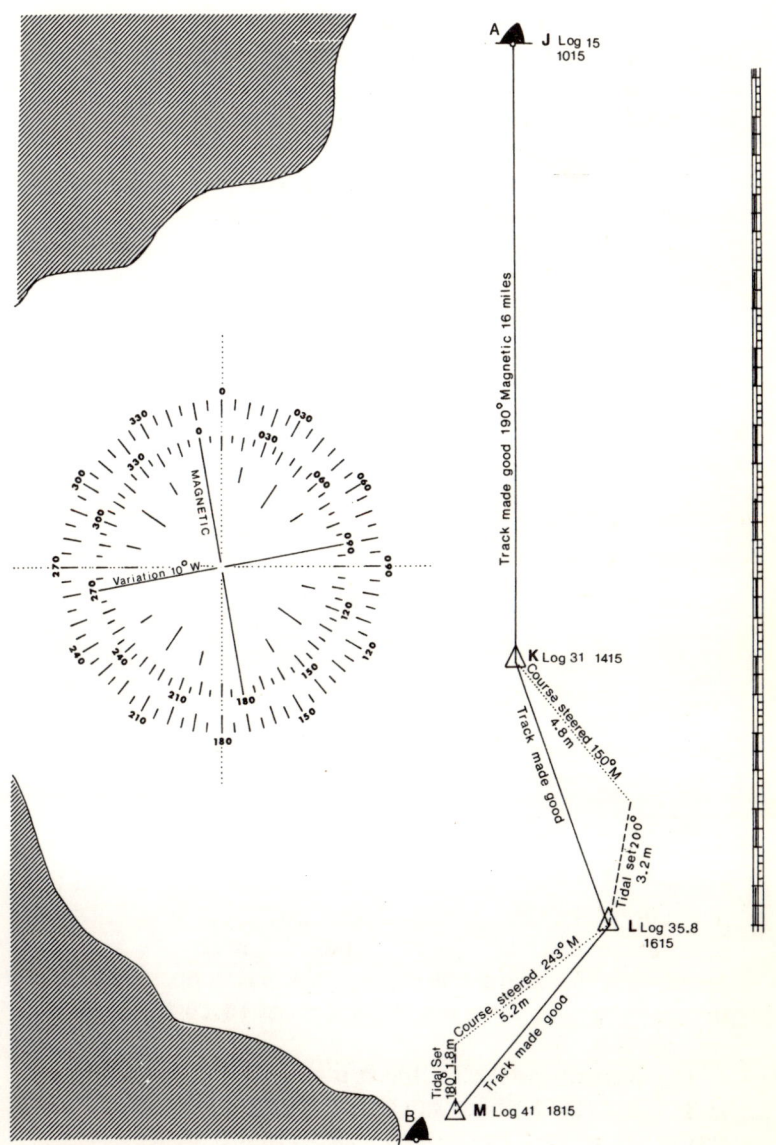

Fig.73 Dead reckoning. Crossing a broad bay. *JKLM* is the track of the boat from 1015 to 1815.

At 14.15 the navigator plots his estimated position. The helmsman reports a course steered of 197° which proved easier in the seas which were quite large earlier on near buoy *A*. 197°, less 3° of leeway and 4° of deviation gives him a magnetic course of 190° and a distance sailed of 16.0 miles. He draws this line on the chart from *J*. During the period the tidal stream cancelled itself out, so his course made good is the line *JK*. At *K* he notes the time, 14.15, and the log reading 31. *K* is his estimated position at 14.15, and is marked with a triangle.

By now the wind has backed further and settles just west of south. The boat can no longer lay her course, so he tells the helmsman to steer close-hauled and to report the course he is managing to steer. He chooses starboard tack because the chartlets for the area show that the favourable tidal stream is stronger offshore than in the bay. An hour later the helmsman reports that he has been averaging 156°, but that he reckons the boat has been making about 4° of leeway. The boat has therefore been making good a course through the water of 152° and this continues during the next hour. At 16.15 the navigator plots on from *K*, his last estimated position. The log reads 35.8 so the boat has covered 4.8 miles through the water.

Course through the water adjusted for leeway	152°
Deviation 2°W	2°
Magnetic course	150°

From *K* he draws a line 4.8 miles, 150° and then, from this line, enters the tidal stream effect, 200°, 3.2 miles. (1.5 miles in the hour 14.15—15.15 plus 1.7 miles 15.15—16.15). Point *L* is his new estimated position, and the track and distance made good from 14.15 to 16.15 is the line *KL*.

The navigator decides that it is time to make an inshore tack, closer to the boat's destination. On port tack she settles on an average course of 242°, but 4° of leeway brings this to a course sailed through the water of 246°. Two hours later, at 18.15, her new estimated position is plotted. The log reads 41, so she has sailed 5.2 miles.

Course through the water	246°
Deviation 3°W	3°
Magnetic course	243°

The course steered is entered, 243°, 5.2 miles. Now the tidal stream which has set the boat 1 mile from 16.15–17.15 and 0.8 miles from 17.15–18.15, a total of 1.8 miles, 180° true. The estimated position at 18.15 is *M*, the track and distance made good from 16.15–18.15 are the line *LM*. At *M*, just over a mile from buoy *B*, he should be able to spot the buoy fine on his port bow and check his position. He should also be able to pick out details on the headland about 1½ miles away.

If it is foggy and he cannot pick up the buoy or the land he would do well to stand out to sea on starboard tack at 17.45 at the latest because a number of errors could have affected his plotting. Suppose that during the first four hours the helmsman had wrongly estimated his course steered and that the boat had been making good 195° instead of 190°, magnetic. The boat's position at 18.15 would not be *M*, but 1½ miles further inshore, about to run aground.

An estimated position is based on approximations and, as such, must be treated with caution. Whenever you are plotting on from an estimated position err on the side of safety. Take a pessimistic view which puts you nearer to any possible danger and plot your onward course accordingly.

Errors There are a number of errors that may creep in to upset the navigator's calculations.

Parallax. If the helmsman is sitting to one side of the compass, and he usually is, the course he thinks he is steering can be several degrees wrong due to parallax. If you have a car with a centrally situated speedometer you will understand the effect if you ask the passenger what speed you are driving at. You will probably disagree as to whether you are inside or outside the speed limit.

Deviation. This can be affected for a while, for example, by a misplaced spanner which puts the boat off course for an hour or so.

The Log. This can be under-registering or over-registering. If you find that the distance you have sailed is unexpectedly greater or less than that registered take an early opportunity to check the log against a measured distance.

Tidal Set and Rate, Seas and Wind. As has already been stated, all the natural elements are variable and can affect your estimated position. It is only through experience that the navigator can make a good estimate of their effects on the boat's performance and course.

Course Steered. It can be as difficult to report to the navigator an average course steered as to tell the driver of a motor car his average speed from watching the speedometer. In heavy seas, for example, the boat will be eased over the waves before returning to her course, and she may eat considerably to windward. Then there are boats with considerable weather helm which are always seeking the wind. Waves can pick up a boat and cause her to surf at great speed, usually off course and covering a considerable distance each time. Running with the wind dead aft the helmsman will tend to point slightly to windward so as to avoid gybing. With a spinnaker set and a small crew he will probably keep the spinnaker full by adjusting his course to the minor changes in wind direction, rather than continually altering the guy and the sheet.

The navigator is wise to check as often as he can the actual course being steered and to judge for himself. The one problem is that he cannot really judge the helmsman's ability to concentrate. If he knows that the navigator is watching him, the helmsman will concentrate hard and steer a much more accurate course. Probably the best answer is for the navigator to stay on deck chatting to him long enough for him to relax his concentration, stealing covert glances at the compass from time to time rather than watching closely the helmsman's every alteration of course.

The Navigator. Don't forget him—he too can make mistakes, especially when cold, wet and tired. He can add deviation when he should be subtracting, he can look up the wrong day or month in the tide table, forget to check whether the tide tables are BST or GMT, he can work on true instead of magnetic. He will make horrible mistakes too—my best was to announce proudly 'there is Hengistbury Head dead ahead', only to realise a minute or two later that we were looking at Portland Bill. But I am sure you will never be over 30 miles out in your landfall!

Planning and Making Passages (1) Take a really good look at the charts first and note all the dangers, oddities of tidal streams, traffic separation zones, navigation marks etc. Work out your optimum course, bearing in mind the likely effects of different winds, possible fog or sudden thunder-storms, and choose as safe a course as possible.

(2) Timing. If you can, arrange to arrive at an unknown destination in daylight.

(3) If the tide is ebbing be extra careful about the depths. It is one thing to chance your arm crossing a bar on a rising tide; to attempt it with barely sufficient water on a falling tide is asking for a postponed cruise at best.

(4) Always plan to make the maximum use of your tidal stream. Often the stream turns inshore much earlier than offshore, so use the fair set offshore as long as possible. Then hug the coast where the adverse set is weakest and you will be well placed to benefit from the first slackening and turning in your favour inshore. In this way when coasting you can get 7 hours favourable and only 5 hours adverse set in a complete cycle.

(5) If your immediate destination is to windward you would normally be wise to tack as nearly as possible within

the area between 5° to either side of the direct course to your destination. You will then be reasonably well placed whether the wind backs or veers.

One exception is when you choose to benefit from a fair tidal stream or to avoid a foul one. When sailing close hauled, progress through the water is relatively slow and the effect of the tidal stream is consequently at its maximum. Unless the rate is very small you will be influenced in your choice of tack by the set and rate of the stream. The forecast too may warn of veering winds in which case you should choose your tack taking this probability into account.

(6) Bearings. Be realistic in your appraisal of your own bearings. If the seas were large or confused, or if you only had a quick sight of a light, treat a bearing with more suspicion than usual and allow a greater margin for error. When you are plotting an onward course from a cocked hat, plot from the corner that is nearest to the danger.

(7) Fog, or poor visibility. Mist or fog can be very long-lasting, but sudden torrential rain can be just as worrying if you are approaching a dangerous coast. At the end of a good few hours out of sight of land and approaching a coast, think well about your plotting if visibility is poor and imagine the maximum cumulative effect of errors. It is probably best to draw a large circle around your last estimated position and to imagine that your boat could be anywhere within it. You may well decide to stay well offshore until visibility improves, and if you do be sure you are not hovering in a shipping lane.

(8) When making a landfall, particularly if the coast is low-lying with very few identifiable objects, aim deliberately upstream of your destination. You then know whether to alter course to port or starboard when you sight the coast, and will have the stream to help you on your way to your harbour.

(9) Before you arrive, check very carefully on the details of the port where you are to moor. If you will be arriving at night be sure you know what the leading lights are, and

have the details of buoyage lighting etc. at your fingertips for reference. Check too on the harbour signals if there is a narrow entrance.

At the end of your cruise, think back on your navigation. We all learn most from experience and observation of crew, boat, wind and sea. All this knowledge is stored away subconsciously at the end of a trip, but the lessons will be learnt all the better and the mistakes made will be recognised if you take your log book and chart home and work through the cruise again. What is more you will find yourself looking forward to your next trip, and to challenging the elements with your ever-increasing skill.

Bon voyage!

Appendix 1

Charthaven

Tide Tables for June   *British Summer Time*

		Metres	Feet			Metres	Feet
1	0609	5.6	18.3	8	0351	1.0	3.2
We	1139	0.8	2.6	We	1052	5.2	17.0
	1828	5.6	18.3		1616	0.9	2.9
	2356	0.7	2.4		2317	5.1	16.9
2	0648	5.7	18.7	9	0444	1.0	3.2
Th	1214	0.7	2.4	Th	1145	5.2	17.0
	1909	5.7	18.7		1713	1.1	3.6
3	0032	0.6	1.9	10	0016	5.0	16.5
Fr	0727	5.8	19.1	Fr	0549	1.1	3.6
	1251	0.6	1.9		1245	4.9	16.2
	1950	5.8	19.1		1829	1.2	4.1
4	0108	0.5	1.8	11	0125	4.9	16.2
Sa	0813	5.9	19.3	Sa	0713	1.2	4.1
	1327	0.4	1.4		1412	4.8	15.7
	2026	5.9	19.3		2002	1.3	4.4
5	0145	0.4	1.4	12	0256	5.0	16.5
Su	0847	5.8	19.1	Su	0851	1.2	4.1
	1408	0.5	1.8		1543	4.9	16.2
	2107	5.8	19.1		2134	1.1	3.6
6	0226	0.6	1.9	13	0424	5.1	16.9
Mo	0928	5.7	18.7	Mo	1012	1.0	3.2
	1437	0.6	1.9		1701	5.0	16.5
	2145	5.6	18.3		2242	1.0	3.2
7	0307	0.8	2.6	14	0521	5.2	17.0
Tu	1007	5.5	18.0	Tu	1110	0.9	2.9
	1529	0.9	2.9		1759	5.3	17.5
	2228	5.4	17.4				

Appendix 2:
Chartlets showing the set and rate of tidal streams for the area depicted in figures 21 and 43.

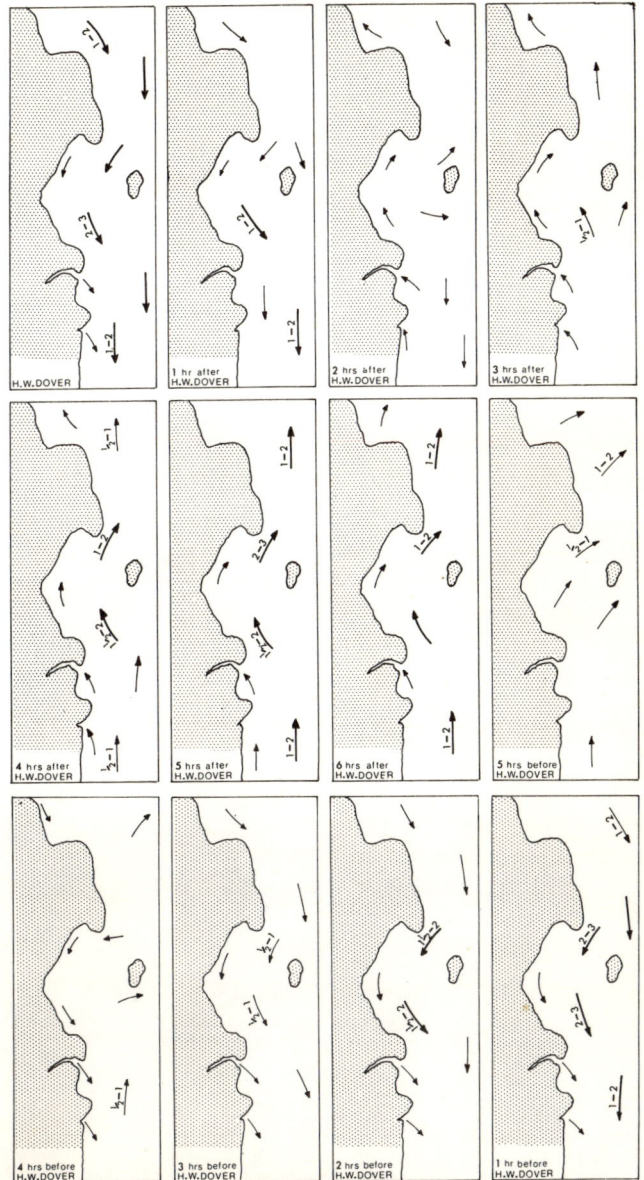

Appendix 3

Sample Deviation Table

Compass heading		Deviation	Magnetic heading
N	0°	3° E	003°
NNE	022½°	4° E	026½°
NE	045°	4° E	049°
ENE	067½°	3° E	070½°
E	090°	2° E	092°
ESE	112½°	1° E	113½°
SE	135°	1° W	134°
SSE	157½°	2° W	155½°
S	180°	3° W	177°
SSW	202½°	4° W	198½°
SW	225°	4° W	221°
WSW	247½°	3° W	244½°
W	270°	2° W	268°
WNW	292½°	1° W	291½°
NW	315°	1° E	316°
NNW	337½°	2° E	339½°

Appendix 4

Sailing directions for yachtsmen

Benest, E.E. *Inland Waterways of Belgium.* Imray, Lawrie, Norie & Wilson.

Benest, E.E. *Inland Waterways of the Netherlands.* Imray, Lawrie, Norie & Wilson.

Blandford, Percy. *Central and southern England.* Regional Sailing Guides: Constable.

Blandford, Percy. *Southern-eastern England.* Regional Sailing Guides: Constable.

Brandon, Robin. *South Biscay Pilot.* Adlard Coles.

Bristow, Philip. *Down the Spanish Coast.* Nautical Publishing Company.

Bristow, Philip. *Through the Belgian Canals.* Nautical Publishing Company.

Bristow, Philip. *Through the French Canals.* Nautical Publishing Company.

Campbell F.S. *Stanford's Harbour Guide to the West Coast of Scotland.*

Clyde Cruising Club Sailing Directions.

Coles, K.A. *Creeks and Harbours of the Solent.* Nautical Publishing Company.

Coles, K.A. *North Brittany Pilot.* Adlard Coles.

Coles, K.A. *Shell Pilot to the South Coast Harbours.* Faber.

Coles, K.A. and Black, A.N. *North Biscay Pilot.* Adlard Coles.

Coote, J.H. *East Coast Rivers.*

Cruising Association Handbook.

Delmar-Morgan, E. *Normandy Harbours and Pilotage.* Adlard Coles.

Delmar-Morgan, E. *North Sea Harbours and Pilotage.* Adlard Coles.

Denham, H.M. *The Adriatic.* John Murray.

Denham, H.M. *The Aegean.* John Murray.

Denham, H.M. *The Ionian Islands.* John Murray.

Denham, H.M. *The Levant and Cyprus.* John Murray.

Denham, H.M. *Southern Turkey.* John Murray.

Denham, H.M. *The Tyrrhenian Sea.* John Murray.

Edwards, L.A. *Inland Waterways of Great Britain.* Imray, Lawrie, Norie & Wilson.

Glazebrook, H. *Anglesey and North Wales Pilot.* Yachting Monthly.

Ireland, East and North Coasts. Irish Cruising Club.

Ireland, South and West Coasts. Irish Cruising Club.

Pooley, D.J. *West Country Rivers.*

Rantzen, M.J. *English Channel Tides.* Adlard Coles.

Townsend, S. *Baltic Pilot.* Adlard Coles.

Wilson, W.E. *Pilots' Guide to the English Channel.* Imray, Lawrie, Norie & Wilson.

Wilson, W.E. *Yachtsman Pilot, Antwerp to Boulogne.* Imray, Lawrie, Norie & Wilson.

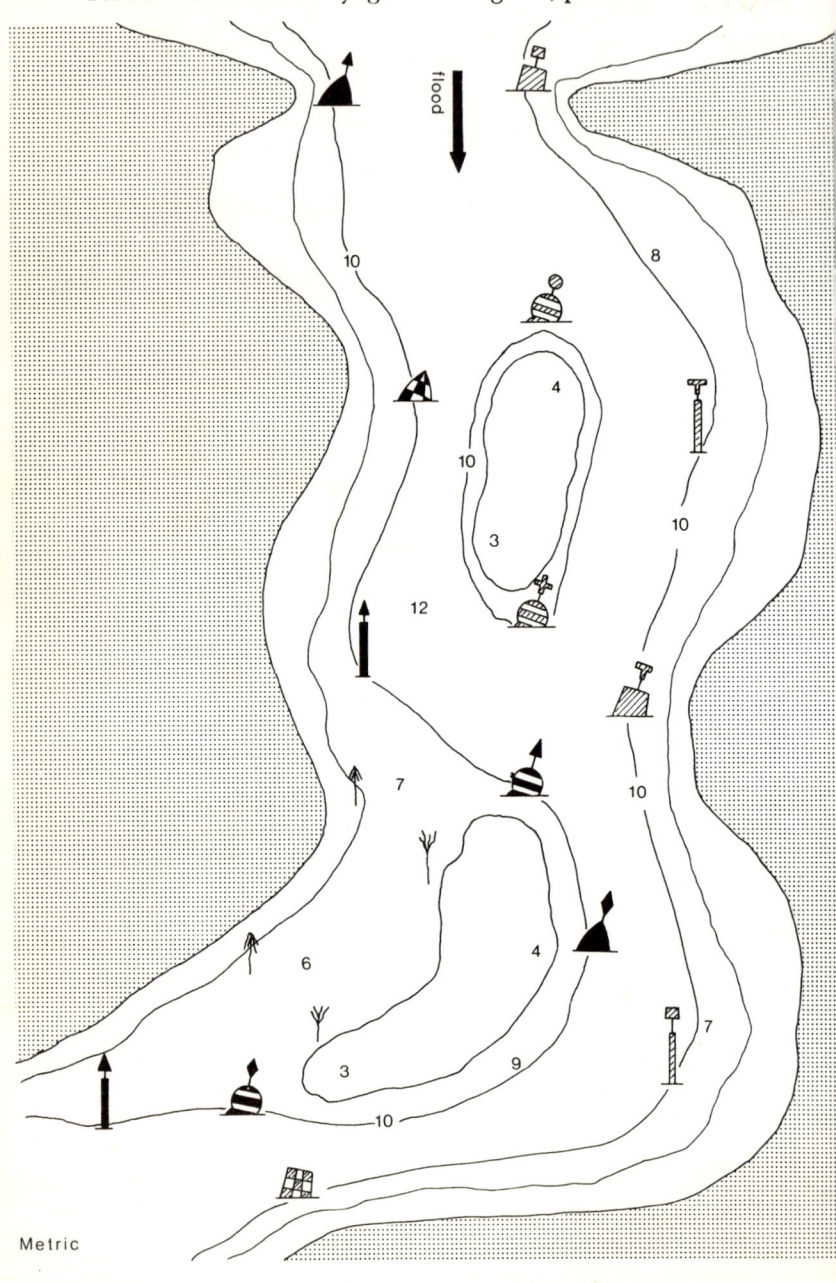

Metric

Index